FRAGMENTS
OF A LESSON PLAN

Let us raise a standard to which the wise and the honest can repair. The event is in the hand of God.

George Washington

What would you think if I sang out of tune,
Would you stand up and walk out on me.
Lend me your ears, and I'll sing you a song,
And I'll try not to sing out of key.

The Beatles

Fragments
Of a Lesson Plan

Robert Belenky

Beacon Press
Boston

This book was written over a period of eighteen years. Many helped,
and I can't possibly name them all. I would like especially to thank the
community people, and the many typists, secretaries, and transcribers
from Harvard, Boston College, and Boston University who sweated
over it. Thank you, everyone, in any way related to the history, events,
or production of this book. To my parents, Max and Sophie, thanks for
good schools and a nice childhood. And Mary, Alice, and Mike—thanks
for everything!

Contents

v

To my teachers . . . in the book and elsewhere

PROLOGUE

September 1970

They went to buy a piglet. We are living in the country now and everything is different from the way it was. We are farmers, you see. Absurd. . .

There is no one to talk to.
There is no one to hear.
I am alone.
The house is quiet.

*   *   *

November 28, 1957

Dearest Mary:

I miss you. Chicago should be closer to New York and when we are married we will make it so. Meanwhile all there is to do is wait.

Graduate school is getting me down. Maybe it's the frustration of being so far apart. Somehow I can't see myself as a researcher—which is what it's all about here. On the other hand, I can't see myself doing therapy. And psychodiagnosis has more limitations than substance.

That doesn't leave me with much of anything, I know. It *would* be nice to find something that I enjoy doing.

Therapy comes closest but in many ways leaves me cold. Besides it feels more than a little dishonest. I can't see charging people from ten to twenty-five dollars an hour for an awkward, insipid conversation.

Is psychotherapy really the big thing?

There are obviously people everywhere who need help, and I grant that there is something about some kinds of inter-personal experiences that often seems to provide such help. At the same time I am not convinced that psychotherapy is more often that kind of experience than not. When I was a swimming counselor at the camp for blind kids at the age of twenty, I think I was a better therapist than I am now, a half-smart, almost-psychologist of twenty-six.

The best psychotherapists are whores. They sell a bit of love and warmth for what the market will bear. Not a bad thing to do. Really rather necessary in this unkind world. But isn't it stretching it a bit to call it a cure and require the whore to be a doctor first?

Okay, so tell me I'm really angry at my great grand-uncle! Where does this leave me?

What will I do with my life?

I don't know. I really don't know.

Maybe camp work in the summer. Group experiences for kids with emotional problems. There are other occupations no doubt but I can't think of them.

Meanwhile I suppose the idea is to get the degree.

There is no question but that psychology is right for me. I love working with people.

My only concern now is to find a place for myself within this rather broad field that could become self-actualizing, socially meaningful, and only slightly phony.

Again, damn it, I can't wait until you get here so we can talk this thing out.

Hurry home. There is so much to do and to talk about and to live for. I hope these next weeks fly by faster than any in our lives. And even if I am a bit skeptical about psychotherapy, I am not about you.

Good-night.

I love you,

Bob

* * *

February 22, 1969

It is with sadness that I threw away some old papers and contemplated the end of an era.

And when you view the past in perspective after so much time you wonder what counted and if anything was learned or could have been—if.

For a living, I profess.

This requires learning . . . or so it is generally presumed.

I profess.

About what?

And to what avail?

(Exactly what are you trying to say that you did?)

But the beautiful dreams return of the utopia in the mountains.

Sullied only by the discrepancy.

(And, come to think of it, what *did* you do?)

Devoid of substance.

(When you finally return to your ivory tower what will you have left behind?)

The students must have known.

(What constructive knowledge? What lasting monument? Will you go back knowing that you did your part?)

And wisely smirked over their dunkles beer at the Wursthaus. Or was it pot?

"Assholes."

"That professor, for example."

"Old fart."

"Out of line. Out of step. Unhip."

"Irrelevant."

"Anti black anti white anti Jew anti Christ."

Ho-hum

(This book would have been much better and there would
have been far less disturbance surrounding it if you had
attempted to work more with the program and concentrated
less on your higher-paying job at the university.)

My courses were exotic. I told them about ordinary people.
(You often imply that we, unlike your friends and colleagues,
are mercurial, benighted, and hostile so that heroes like yourself would seem to deserve a medal for jungle duty.)

Don't you see?

We are *all* exotic

Equally so

Equally so

But who is the traveller?

* * *

Chapter One

TROUBLE IN SCHOOL

November 3, 1965
Bostonians elected the wrong school committee yesterday.
Mrs. Louise Day Hicks got in by a fantastic margin. Badly
planned campaign by the good guys. Negroes and white
liberals, who constitute together no more than maybe fifteen
percent of the vote, did nothing but scream "de facto segre-
gation!" Not a very likely slogan to inspire majority Irish
Catholic support. Yet the schools in *their* neighborhoods
are also terrible and with proper publicity these conditions
could have been exposed and a progressive Negro-Irish
coalition for educational improvement might have been
welded. The Boston schools are lousy for *everyone* and only
in that sense democratic.

Harry Collins,* Teen-Age Aide
My brother was causing trouble in school.
  It started this way: He used to bring a whole lot of stolen
food, sweets, candy, and everything like that that the teacher
didn't approve of. The teachers thought that since I was the
oldest I set the example for him. I told the teacher that I
didn't and he said, "Yes you do!"

  *Names followed by an asterisk (*) are not the real names
of persons involved. The asterisk will be used only on the first occur-
rence of the name.

1

One day I played hooky from school. I came the next day. When I went into school, the teacher asked me where I been. I told him I wasn't feeling good. I guess he knew I was lying. He told me to sit down. I noticed my brother was crying. We were in the same class. I said, "What's wrong with my brother?" He was crying so bad and everything. The teacher said, "Look at his hands." I looked at his hands and saw the marks on them.

I asked the teacher, "Why did you do that?" Then he came over to where I was and said, "What did you say?"

I told him, "Don't you ever do that to my brother again!"

So he started hitting on me with a stick, a long piece of skinny stick — they call it a rattan. He hit me across my face and I wouldn't take it. So I got up out of my seat and hit him on the side of the jaw. I know I did wrong but I was mad.

Then after that he ran out of the room and got some other teacher. They started holding me, grabbing me, and hitting me. My teacher hit me all over my face. Then he told me to get out of school and never come back.

I told that teacher I was going to get him. I told my friends to wait for me. I was not going to take it no more! The teacher thought I was fooling with him. The minute he hit the curb for a red light one of my friends snatched him out of the car and we started beating him up and everything. The next day he had the cops waiting for me when I came to school.

I tried going to school again but the teacher made it hard on me. He finally got me thrown out for good. I was fifteen years old.

* * *

Arthur Davis, Teen-Age Aide
If I only stayed there.
If I had stayed in Georgia I'd be finished with school by now.

I'd probably be finished with school by now.
Some people have it hard, very hard.
Some people have it harder than this.
I seen kids with snow on the ground going
Ice on the ground
Zero degrees
Going to school
No seat on their pants
Barefooted
No hat on their head
No coat
But still in there trying to make it.
Those are people I really feel for.
Those are people my heart really has love for.
Sometimes I wish I could really help them.
But looking at myself
I can't help myself
I just can't help myself
I see the kids people laugh at
But, me, I never did
I always felt sorry for them because I knew their mother did
    the best they could.
They're trying to go to school to get something out of life
And these are people who really need it.
A lot of people don't see this.
A lot of people don't give it a thought.
They want you to come to school.
That's all the teachers really think about
And that's all the principal thinks about.
Come to school.
They don't care how you come
But come to school
If you don't come to school
They're going to send somebody to make you come to school
Those are the kids that really need caring for

3

Really need feeling for.
They don't have to give them money to come to school
Just pick them up in a bus
So they can come to school
Barefooted
No clothes on their backs
In cold weather.
Sometimes I used to give kids my coat
And a regular sweater
To keep them warm.
Small kids with raggedy clothes on scares you
Yet they're trying to get something out of life
And still can't get nowhere.
That's why I ain't got nothing, I reckon
That's why I ain't got nothing.
I feel for other people.
A lot of times I had to go like that myself
Cold,
Hungry . . .
But it didn't matter
I wanted to learn.
When you see what some kids go through
You say to yourself,
"Why, why do some kids have to be rich and some kids have
    to be poor?"
"Why can't they be equal?"
Oh, I'm thinking about it.
I'm thinking about it everyday.
I have been cheated and I know it.
I know I've been cheated from the first time I started going
    to school.
I know I haven't been treated fair
But yet, and still I took it.
Not only me.
Not only myself

But a lot of other people haven't been treated fair.
That's why I never speak for myself.
There's more people that may be in worse condition than I
    am
And I know a lot of people that is.

                * * *

Last night I spoke to one of the Boston School System's
assistant superintendents. It now seems certain that they
will *not* permit me to volunteer consultant time to their
guidance service. The word seems to have gotten around that
I am a dangerous fellow who should be stayed clear of. This
bugs me. The reason: I introduced some controversy into last
summer's Harvard-Boston Summer School Program.

                * * *

How groovy to be thought of as so dangerous that you're
blackballed by a major city school system. How effective.
Batman, the Green Hornet, Robin Hood, Stenka Razin. But
on the other hand it's absurd. My offenses: 1) Noel Day, a
black intellectual, was invited as a guest speaker and was
boycotted by the Boston School personnel; 2) Jean Oxley, a
great black lady to whom they had given tenure, presumably
by mistake, was hired as an instructor over their objections;
3) I called Mr. What's-His-Name, their principal, "racially
motivated" when he supposed that our Neighborhood Youth
Corps kids were irresponsible without knowing them
personally; 4) I told a joke one hot evening when we had a
parent's program at the school. There were about ten big-
shot speakers and me. I was last. . .just about asleep. So
there was this teacher who was rambling on and the little boy
in the class raised his hand . . . "Yes, Billy," she said.

5

"Teacher, may I go 'we-we'?" "No, Billy, recess isn't until eleven thirty." Minutes pass. Hand is raised. "Please, teacher, I must go 'wee-wee.' " "No, etc." More minutes pass. Hand again. "Please, please, please, teacher. I must, must, must go 'wee-wee' or I shall truly burst." "Well, all right, Billy, you may go 'wee-wee.' " Billy gets up, stretches, and goes "Whee! Whee!" Those who were there said that the expression on the face of Miss Margaret Sullivan (age: geologic), very influential, second in command of the school system, was ashen, disapproving, scandalized. So henceforth it was decreed that I am to be banned from Boston. This incident (series of) gives me at least some small credibility in the black community when they hear (and I tell them). There were other incidents since, and now they accuse me of masterminding things I never heard of. Oh, it's groovy.

* * *

Doc: What about the school scene? What's it like?

Kids: It's too boring.

It's just a blah, you know. Like you could take it or leave it.

Like a cigarette. I haven't been to school for about three or four months. Most of the kids lost interest in school, no parents or anything, and now they're putting a new law out, you either get suspended or you get the stick. They break a stick over your hand.

Five times on each hand.

If you don't take the stick you get suspended. But if you get suspended you get a D for the marking period.

That ain't no choice.

Like they got a bench down there. You don't go to

6

school to sit on a bench.

The school Billy goes to, this teacher, Mr. Konig,*
I was fooling around with a kid then he started
rough and I got rough. He didn't do nothing to the
other kid cause the kid was colored, right? He just
picked *me* up by my neck and smashed me up
against the wall.

The teachers these days are more like wrestlers.
They just don't understand the kids. They're too
emotional. They beat you, punch you in the
mouth. That's what they do. They take you in a
room and they beat you. Where no one can hear it.
I had a problem in school. I had a hard time with
reading. Like I couldn't stand sitting down doing
my homework. I still can't stand it. Every single
day I'd be out in the hall, getting the stick, every
single day, three or four times, for like swearing at
the teacher, throwing a book at him.

"You know, I ain't doing this shit."

"Get outta here. Get out in the hall."

"Yeah, okay, yeah."

Two or three times on each hand. I walk back in
the room laughing.

"You think it's funny? Get out in the hall again!"
Believe me, man. That stick would fucking hurt
after a while.

It would aggravate you. It aggravated me so much
that I quit school.

Like they had social workers or some shit like that
at the school. Other guys would get sent down to
talk to them. I never explained any of my problems to them. I don't think it would have helped
me out if I did.

That bastard said, "I'm going to get the fucking
stick." I said,

"Fuck the stick."

I was going to get the stick from the gym teacher, right? I got so terrified of getting the stick, I fucking quit school the day before I was going to get the stick off him. And I got the stick off all the other teachers in that school and it blew my fucking mind, man. I couldn't take it no more. So I went out and started getting fucked up. So the next year I think it was I ended up in fucking prison.

I got the stick twice by Mr. Johnson.* Once he broke the stick on my fingers and that hurt. That hurt like a bastard. And the second time. He did it about four times on each hand. My hands were real sore, you know. My fingers started to get blisters and all that shit.

Some teachers in there got the strength, you know. They get like a fourteen-year-old kid. They hit him once. WHACK! He starts screaming.

"Put your hand out!"

"NO! No. No. PLEASE!"

* * *

Anonymous Note: March, 1968
> BELENKY —
> PLEASE KEEP YOUR MOUTH SHUT ABOUT
> CORPORAL PUNISHMENT IN THE SCHOOLS.
> YOU DON'T KNOW WHAT THE HELL YOU'RE
> TALKING ABOUT! HAVE THE DECENCY TO
> THINK ABOUT THE REPUTATION OF BOSTON
> COLLEGE AT LEAST!!!!!!!

* * *

Article: *The Jewish Advocate*, Thursday,
March 21, 1968

On Wednesday, March 13, I attended a hearing of the
Joint Education Committee, which was considering
several bills designed to outlaw corporal punishment in the schools of the Commonwealth. Being
present at such an occasion is a bizarre and un-
forgettable experience, but one which, for all its
unpleasantness, I would heartily recommend to all
citizens. Witness after witness stood before the
committee to make serious statements in favor of
the proposed legislation and each without excep-
tion was harassed and insulted by each committee
member. There seemed to be little purpose in this
behavior except to disrupt the proceedings which
the committee itself had initiated.

It became clear soon enough that the committee
had no interest in learning anything at all about
punishment, corporal or otherwise and was simply
determined at any cost to discredit those who even
in the mildest way threatened the status quo within the Commonwealth's educational establishment.
I quickly "lost my cool." Although I had not
planned to testify and had nothing prepared, the
whole procedure bothered me so much that I felt
that I just *had* to say something. So I did and was
of course cut down like everyone else.

* * *

The day after the hearing I got a call from a big shot in the
Boston Public Schools. He said, "Belenky, get your goddamned
program out of the Campbell School."

* * *

The next day I got a copy of a letter which a moderately well-respected psychologist wrote to the chairman of that legislative committee:

Dear Senator Fonseca:

I would like to express my own feeling of apology to you and the members of the committee on Education for the behavior of my fellow psychologist, Dr. Belenky. I want to assure you that the kinds of feelings expressed by my colleague do not represent those of the profession. For example, I am a member of a Boston Ward Democratic Committee and have served as a ward coordinator for local and state-wide candidates. As I was at the hearing representing the Massachusetts Psychological Association, I felt particularly concerned.

I am hopeful that future confrontations between psychologists and you and the members of your Committee shall be more fruitful than the recent encounter.

Sincerely yours,
Dr. K ____

I answered:

Dear Senator Fonseca:

"I would like to express my own feeling of apology to you and the members of the Committee on Education for the behavior of my fellow psychologist Dr. K ____ . I want to assure you that the embarrassing lack of articulateness and commitment in his dryly "professional" testimony does not represent the orientation of a large segment of our profession. As I was at the hearing at the request of the New Urban League of Boston, I felt particularly concerned.

I am hopeful that future confrontations between psychologists and you and the members of your

10

committee shall be more forceful and enlightening.
With the collaboration of professionals I hope that
the community can bring pressure to bear upon
you which will lead ultimately to more humane
conditions in our schools.

Sincerely yours,
Dr. B ___

Ha! (The gadfly strikes again.)

* * *

March 8, 1968
Dear Bob:
If you wish a reason for this action it is because
you do not seem to want to fit into our system or
pattern. . . . This is not intended as any criticism,
just as a statement that your way of doing things
does not fit into the overall pattern that is best for
our department.

Yours truly,
Bill

* * *

October, 1967

The Compulsory Tearoom
It was a difficult and delicate role. And I blew it.

The reform school was in the country amid trees and
flowers, a lake used for swimming in the summer. The trees
were alive with brilliant red, orange, yellow. The sun seemed
to hang low over everything, and the days remained myste-
riously warm during that whole fall. The inmates, young girls
who must have been pretty, in prison-blue smocks, strangely

11

lacking animation, gliding with forced purpose across the manicured New England campus.

No one was actually cruel — as far as I could see — but rather proper.

Ate with the headmistress in the dining hall — lunch faultlessly served by an inmate. (And as the women came and went we discussed art and literature and shit like that.) The assistant headmistress was sort of Fabian socialist. Favored a minimal subsidized income. Very cultivated.

Many of the girls never had it so good. Sheets on the bed for the first time and predictable meals. I learned that they each had a private room. Later discovered that they were actually cells, locked at night and returned to under key when no formal activity was scheduled. The staff had a dreadful fear of homosexuality. So the inmates needed to be protected from unplanned, unsupervised, unspied-upon human contact.

(They later put a stern-faced matronly spy in my therapy group to "assist." At least one kid got in trouble for what she said in "therapy.")

* * *

Dorothy: Oh, will you help me? Can you help me?

Good Witch: You don't need to be helped any longer.
             You've always had the power to go back to Kansas.

Dorothy: I have?

* * *

January, 1967
Being locked up. Going on my third day. In a freezing, cold room. You sleep in there. Look at four walls. They don't give you nothing but one blanket.

(Dorothy* is fourteen years old. Popular with the staff. Lancaster Training-Reform-School. The kids like her, too. She seems younger. Active, bouncy. Cute. She's homeless and gets into trouble on the outside. Nothing serious. She's homeless.)

(The room. Just a rubber mattress and a wooden block for the mattress to go on. A little window with chicken wire. And a pail. And a door and nothing else but four walls.)

(It was a cold day in January. Her hands were blue.)

They got nothing in there. You're not even supposed to have a book to read. It's freezing! It's an icebox. One blanket. One.

I told the matron off. It started in the dining room. I came out from clearing the dishes. The tray fell a funny way and I caught it and everybody started laughing and the matron came up and she said, "Oh, you want an audience! She's got an audience now. She's happy."

I said, "I don't want no audience."

She said, "Now watch her make a scene."

So I kind of pushed the girl next to me to read my lips and I went, "You don't bother me, bitch!"

The matron read my lips and she screamed, "You don't bother *me* neither!" Then she said, "You got anything to say to me, say it out loud!"

I said, "I cannot stand your living guts and never could!" I said, "I cannot stand you! I *hate* you!!"

She chased me upstairs and I got mad and threw all my stuff on the floor. Some bottles broke. So I got a dustpan and a broom to clean it up. She screamed, "Put it back!"

I said, "Well, I *need* it."

She said, "You're going into solitary confinement!"

I ran down the kitchen and I came upstairs and the kids were dragging me. I was crying. They threw me into solitary.

Then she took me out. She said, "That's just to show you I *can* put you in there." She laughed. And then she put me in again.

13

She starts it. She starts it all the time with me. She *likes* me, you know. See, she's trying to get me out of the habit of swearing and everything. But you know, I just want to be a tomboy.

> ("No one really explained the mission, but from what I heard from the men, it was suspected that these villagers were Viet Cong sympathizers . . .")

My girl friend. Betsey,* she was in there a week straight on peanut butter sandwiches and milk and when they got her out of there, she was like *this* — like a bone. Then they forced her to eat and you know then she got sick and everything.

No windows at all. There's all bugs and things in the beds and everything. Some kids been down there a month.

> ("As they moved in closer to the village, they just kept shooting at people. I remember this man distinctly, holding a small child in one arm and another child in the other, walking toward us . . .")

Feel like you want to scream. Feel like you're in a mad house. I wouldn't put a dead dog in that room. I wouldn't.

> ("They saw us and were pleading.")

If I had a child that was bad, I'd put him in a room. But I'd have it so it's heated. I'd rather beat a kid than lock him in that room. That ice cube. I'd kill my kid before I'd put him in that room.

> ("The little girl was saying 'no, no' in English. . . .")

I wouldn't lock my own kid up if I had one. I wouldn't do that. I'd just sit there and listen to him. I'd take in the feelings, you know, and see just what bothers him. When he's got it all out, I'd say, "What started it all? You tell me your side of it." And if he don't want to tell it, let him sit there daydreaming. That's one of the best things a child or anyone can do is daydream. They figure daydreaming strengthens the mind. It shows the way of what you want for a future, what you really need, what you really feel. But. . . .

14

("Then all of a sudden a burst of fire and they
were cut down. All of these people in the big
circle and they were trying to run . . . ")

Solitary doesn't help. It makes you even worse, just looking at the doorway. All you do is look at the door and you go
crazy.

I don't care about nothing. I might not even be living in
five or ten years but I want to get out of this place, go to a
regular school, graduate, go into the telephone business.
Settle down, have kids, a husband and lead a life. Not the life
I been leading here.

("A guy with an M16 fired at them, at the four-
year-old, and the five-year-old fell over to protect
the smaller boy . . . Then they fired six more shots
and just let them lie.")

I know that the state senate is investigating this place and
I hope they tear it down because it *needs* to be torn down.
But I don't think the senate is going to do anything. I don't
think it's going to close it down. Because it's going to take a
lot of people to close this place down, to tear it down.

("I left the village around 11 o'clock that morning.
I saw clumps of bodies and I must have seen as
many as a hundred killed. It was done very
businesslike.")

* * *

Oh, I burst furiously into print.

MILD MANNERED PSYCHOLOGIST FOR A GREAT
METROPOLITAN UNIVERSITY BARES RED PAJAMAS!!

(Actually it was a gentleman's protest; reasonable, professional, and ineffective.)

"The sight of adolescents locked in their unheated rooms
for several daylight hours and throughout the night would
bother me even if I were not a trained psychologist. Placing

15

young girls in prolonged solitary confinement for a week, two weeks, a month would anger me.

"Allowing children no one with whom they can talk about real or imagined problems without fear of official reprisal would offend my sense of what is fair and right.

"My major use was so that it could be said 'We have a psychologist,' even though I was not treated as a professional.

"My only usefulness to the Lancaster girls now is in talking freely and openly about their institution in the hope that enlightened public opinion will bring about reform.

"In so doing, I feel I am carrying out my professional duty to my clients."

There were television interviews, radio discussions, anonymous letters, incredulous comments by members of the profession. Brou. ha. ha. It was too easy. "My professional duty!" I should have *stayed*, dammit! I should have forced them to let me stay. And from that pulpit screamed and bellowed enlightenment!

A fellow named Dr. Tartakoff (who was my boss, they told me, although I saw him first at the time of crisis), listened sympathetically to my tale of abuses. I gave him an impassioned speech, bringing in Nazi doctors who viewed their professions technically, licked the ass that fed them, and did untold human damage. He might have seen the resemblance because he was a decent fellow and probably a liberal. He told me that he would not fire me. I breathed a sigh of relief. "But," he added, "I forbid you ever to return to Lancaster and I shall withhold your salary indefinitely."

How do you fight that? So I went to the papers. I quit rather than be fired. Took the tack of indignation for the sake of the inmates. That was the critical mistake. I should have fought like a wolf to remain and, had they fired me, I should have returned as a volunteer with a fleet of reporters and a ragtag army of the unworthy poor.

E. Z. Friedenberg once in a *Saturday Review* critique of

Kozol's exposé, *Death at an Early Age*, roundly attacked Jonathan for not providing the kids with a model of a successful fighter, because from their point of view Kozol was ultimately defeated and forced to leave them, whining brave rhetoric. The same applies to me. Heroism is cheap outside of jail.

* * *

Chapter Two

PLAYROOM 81

(From a paper given at the New England Personnel and
Guidance Association meetings, October 1966, Bretton
Woods, N.H. Published in "Occasional Papers," Harvard
Graduate School of Education, 1967.)

October 4, 1966
Mrs. Faith Harding: It started about a year ago when the
Harvard group came into our neighborhood – Dr.
Robert Belenky, Mr. Jonathan Clark, and Mr. James
Reed. They were approached with suspicion, you
know. They wanted to find out just really what
was needed in the part of Roxbury where we
live – the Mission Hill housing project. And, of
course, most of the mothers said, "A place for our
children to play." You see there is no play area
there and about two thousand families but no place
for the children.

So we started up a program called "Playroom 81."
It consists of ten mothers from the neighborhood –
two white mothers from the other side of the project
and the rest of them are Negro.

We used the basement of the building at 81
Prentiss Street. It was very dingy – just a project
basement. We had meetings every day to plan just

what we should do. The first thing was to beautify the basement. We all got together and worked on that. The management of the project put tile on the floor. Soon it was just pretty — for the children. There's no use for children to come from one miserable place to another. We made it pretty for them so they could feel more at ease.

We have children of all ages coming down to the Playroom now — three-and-a-half-year-olds to twelve-year-olds. The preschoolers stay around all day and the older ones come in after school. We have a little harder time with them because we capture them when they come out of school. And they're raring to go! You know, they're pent up all day. Try keeping a female all day without talking, well, that's against nature already! But the boys were even *more* raring to go. It is difficult but we manage.

They come in at three o'clock and we have arts and crafts — in any line that they like. We have one mother who teaches cooking. I was surprised to find that a lot of the children don't know how to cook. I don't believe their mothers let them cook anything. The children thought that it was quite something to learn to bake and make different things. And we have a sewing class. All of these activities might go on at the YMCA or someplace but most of the children we have are young and they can't go out of the community by themselves. We have given them a place to come and we're very proud of it because the mothers themselves put a lot of work into it and it's known around the community. The children themselves like to come down because it's their place.

Another thing that we're trying to do is this:

You see, we're between two projects, a white project *here* and a colored project *here*. Only a street separates them but people won't cross it. We did get two mothers from the Mission — the white project — and they fit in very well. I believe that they discovered after being there that we all had the same things in mind and were trying to make the same strides. I don't think that their children had ever played with colored children before but the children got along fine, too.

We also developed a baby-sitting service because most of the mothers in the community don't have any place to leave their children if they have an emergency — like going to a hospital clinic — so we started that service in the mornings. We are expanding in a number of ways and this is one of them.

The poverty program people (Action for Boston Community Development) were interested. You see, none of the mothers had any training at all and with just a little bit of money we did a lot of things. They think that if we mothers got a salary and further training, there's a lot more that we could do. We could begin a training process at the Playroom so other mothers can learn about programs for children and go on to other jobs in this particular line.

* * *

October 3, 1966
Holy Sodom and Gomorrah, Batman, these guidance counselors are indistinguishable from Rotarians!

We're up in Bretton Woods, New Hampshire, in the most elegant of ancient hotels, convening with the pupil personnel establishment. What they lack in wit and substance, they make up in merriment. And, by Jesus, they're not only white, they're a bunch of bloody Christians! Invocation and benediction at dinner were given by a priest in the name of Christ.

And apart from our own Mrs. Faith Harding, there is nary a brown, let alone a black, face to be seen. Well, no, there *was* a soft-shoe song-and-dance man included in last night's borscht-circuit musicale.

I have really never seen anything like it! Best-sounding meeting was mediocre and attended by only twelve. But the waiters did a dance with sparklers while serving the dessert and there were parties all night everywhere. Drunks were to be found on the staircase in the morning.

* * *

Audience: Who did you say does the teaching in these art and crafts and cooking classes?

Mrs. Harding: The mothers. The children are divided into age groups. I have the seven- and eight-year-olds. Each mother has age groups like that and has classes for them every day. The mothers themselves do the teaching.

Audience: Are they volunteers?

Mrs. Harding: They were volunteers at first. We are now getting eighty dollars a month from the Commonwealth Service Corps (a kind of state-run VISTA program). So I guess you might say that we're still volunteers. Between October, 1965 and January 1966, mothers came down from ten in the morning until five at night for no money. In January the Commonwealth Service Corps stepped in and saw what we were trying to do and gave the mothers a little encouragement to go on. The money did help a lot. The program is much better now than when it started. The children went on trips this summer to places that I've never been to myself. They enjoyed a good summer. I think that we did a lot to prepare them for school, so they can make better progress. I think that the program is moving along.

Belenky: I want to relate what Mrs. Harding has said to some of the ideas about guidance and school psychology that some of us have been working on. I would like us to consider Mrs. Harding's description of Playroom 81 as a model for the kinds of activities that might well be generated by school-related mental health workers. The guidance professions — I am including within this rubric, school psychology, counseling, as well as vocational and college guidance — have traditionally concentrated their efforts on assessment and appropriate placement whether in school grade, curriculum, college, or job. Increasingly, however, schools have become aware of marginal clients — notably nonlearners and overly aggressive children. It has become the task of the guidance staff to deal with them, however ineffectively. Habitually, the counselor has worked with each case separately, using group methods on occasion. However, it is only if he asks the question: "Why are there more school failures and 'adjustment' problems in some neighborhoods than in others?" that he is in a position to view the task on a social-psychological rather than on an individual basis, gaining thereby considerable leverage. He might then be able to entertain the possibility that there is something wrong with the way in which the school is dealing with its clients taken as a whole — the way in which the school as an institution is making sense to those it purports to serve.

In Boston, as in most large American cities, education is antiquated and open school-community tensions abound. We decided therefore not to work under the aegis of the school system. But whether the bureaucrats knew it or liked it or not, we were determined to serve the system's clients in order to make schools more effective and education more vital — in at least one Boston neighborhood. Our belief was that by involving local parents in the process of learning, by helping them indeed to become *educators,* we might generate real educational progress with the sanction, indeed the active thrust, of the community. We are not talking about "selling" education as presently constituted; instead we are talking about a collaborative development, a collaboration which ultimately may have to be sold to or forced upon the present school establishment. However, once the school and community work together effectively and the school begins to function in its rightful role as the community's agent — in the same sense that a doctor or lawyer is the agent of a given client — it is reasonable to predict that learning and "adjustment" problems will not continue to exist in their present form or virulence. It may *then* make sense to try to handle them on a case basis.

We are therefore proposing that the guidance worker be hired by some agency — a school, a settlement house, a university, or a private community group — to generate pro-educational activities, such as Playroom 81, which will have the effect of broadening participation in and therefore commitment to learning and teaching functions and will also ultimately have the effect of modifying the school's contract with its clients.

It has been very difficult to study what we have been doing in a scientific sense because our "subjects" — Mrs. Harding is one — are entirely aware of the nature of the "experiment." Therefore the biasing effect is no doubt enormous. However, I think that these results may be pointed to thus far: 1. The morale of the mothers has increased; 2. Their feelings of competence and self worth have increased; 3. They've become more sophisticated about education both through in-service seminars and through trips to schools in Boston and New York; 4. A sense of optimism about what can happen in education has been generated. While organizationally their group has some weaknesses and they have not yet had a direct effect on the local schools, strides are being made in both directions. They are soon to be, I believe, articulate spokesmen of their community to the schools, very much like suburban PTA ladies but hopefully on a more sophisticated and vigorous level.

Audience: Mrs. Harding, do you have many men involved in your program?

Mrs. Harding: We don't have many fathers involved because it's a neighborhood with a lot of broken homes so there's no fathers to *be* involved. It's a suspicious neighborhood because, you see, the people have been told so many times to come on up to this meeting or that place and such and such will be done and then nothing happens. Well, people get tired of hearing these things. Then when something really and truly comes along, they're not interested. It's like crying wolf. But there are a lot of *women* who are concerned about the children and what is going on in the community. They come around to see what's going with the program. But there's not too many men that are involved, although we could really use them.

Audience: How many children come to the Playroom?

Mrs. Harding: We have eighty-five signed up and about forty come down each day.

Audience: Are many mothers using the facility for baby-sitting?

Mrs. Harding: They are not taking advantage of that as much as they should. Boy, I have six children and I wish something like this was going on a long time ago.

Belenky: Mrs. Harding spoke of community attitudes. She spoke of suspicion. There is also the feeling of self-worth or lack of it reinforced everywhere. A kid comes to school with the expectation that it's going to be rough and he's going to fail. It *is* rough and he *does* fail. He then becomes not simply someone who has failed, but a *failure*. With the men jobless-ness leads to the same sense of failure. Really, *everyone* is at the mercy of welfare agencies, the schools, the housing authority, and creditors. All this leads to a kind of endemic depression and doubt about competence — competence to hold a job, competence to read a book and get something out of it, competence to keep control of one's children, competence to make a plan and execute it. A program — any program — which allows people to act on their own ideas and do something elegant on their own behalf is bound to change this expecta-tion. A gradual movement toward optimism about oneself will hopefully occur. Is this not consistent with the traditional goals of guidance?

Audience: Have you seen signs of these changes in self-confidence?

Belenky: We have done some intensive interviewing of the mothers. Frequently they talk about how "I used to be just a simple housewife who did the dishes and watched television all day long and now I

discover that I can add something to the community." Some tell us that they've discovered
that they're smarter than they used to think. This
kind of anecdote comes up time and time again.
Audience: Have you gotten any feedback from the school?
Mrs. Harding: We haven't, no, but they know we're there.
Some of the teachers have come down to see what
we're doing. But we haven't had any focus yet
concerning that.
Audience: Is there any evidence that children have changed
in their attitudes toward school?
Mrs. Harding: Well, I haven't noticed any, really. I don't
know what we can do down in the Playroom to give
them a different approach to school when they have
to go back to that same routine. I think that our role
is to give them something to do when they come out
of school and try to put them into a little better
frame of mind. I think that's the best we can do.
Belenky: This may be a long time in coming everywhere but
the elementary guidance counselor can certainly
help simply by getting to know his community and
striving to bring learning into focus by, oddly
enough, facilitating political cohesion. He should, I
think, wander about the neighborhood and get to
know the children, the adults, and the prevalent
attitudes and issues. If he is an employee of the
school, it should be his job to be the school's
change agent in order, as it were, to make these
attitudes and issues central parts of the curriculum.

*   *   *

January 13, 1966
This is Jim Reed. I want to record some of the things that are
going on here at Playroom 81. It's three-thirty and we've just

26

opened up the Playroom for the afternoon. The tables are all laid out. This is a long dark, dirty basement in the Mission Hill Extension Housing Project. But it's very lively now.

Down at the far end of the room Gail Titus, a teen-age aide, has a group of young girls whom she calls the Missionettes. She's working with them sort of isolated from the rest of the kids. They are playing some sort of quiet game. Four of the girls are present — all about twelve or thirteen years old.

We have about twenty kids here now and a littly puppy. Gail is trying to keep the puppy under control.

Four large tables have been set up for the kids. Josephine Lopes, another of our teen-age aides, has some children around a table and she has some pencils and paper and she and the kids are busy drawing.

Right next to me in the library area Arthur Davis, another aide, is talking with a small boy. Arthur is a beautiful guy. Let's listen in.

Arthur: How old are you?
Boy: Five.
Arthur: You go to school?
Boy: Yes, at the Ira Allen.
Arthur: Tell me something. Do you like your school?
Boy: No.
Arthur: You don't? Really? Tell me why.
Boy: Hit you on the hand.
Arthur: Why do they hit you on the hand?
Boy: For being bad.
Arthur: Don't you think you *deserve* being hit on the hand
          if you're bad?
Boy: Yeh.
Arthur: Are there some other things you don't like about
          school?
Boy: Having to do a lot of work.

27

Arthur: Oh. What do you want to be when you grow up?

Boy: Superman.

Arthur: How can you be Superman if you don't go to school? How can you get to be anything if you don't go to school? If you don't go to school you'll just never be nothing. Look, the teacher hit you because you do something wrong, right? So if you don't do nothing wrong, she won't hit you, right?

Another one of our aides, Tony Addison, is looking at toys with some children. He has them busy making decisions about what they will do.

The door is opening and other kids are coming in and they, too, will be placed with their teen-age group leaders. The kids coming in seem to know exactly with whom they are to work and where they should go. There's a fine degree of order so far.

I'm going to walk around to some of the tables and we're going to listen to what some of the young people are saying. First we'll go to Tony's table.

Tony: I'm not going to take no foolishness out of none of you. This is going to be a *good* group. Like I said, if you want anything, you can ask me and I'll get it for you. If there are any arguments, come to me and I'll settle them. No running around. All right? Is that clear?

Now we're going to listen to what Miss Josephine Lopes is doing. She's writing on a pad and a little girl is reading.

Little girl: "I thought the high school was very nice. It is nice, but, oh, how I miss my friends. It is too bad . . . "

28

Josephine, it seems, is tutoring the little girl in reading. She is playing a reading game with her. Now here I am beside Gail and her Missionettes.

Gail: All right, if them girls don't start coming regular I'm just going to have to get some other girls. We won't start our meeting today until all the girls are here.

Girl: What about the trip?

Gail: Well, yeah. You girls want to go on a trip tomorrow. I'm going to come with you after school. And you all are going to cooperate and go out like I told you to and quit fooling around. You're going to act like young ladies and not like five-year-old kids who run around and do this or that like a chicken with its head cut off!

The count has now come up to thirty-nine children. I'm going to walk out front now to the door and see what's going on out there. Here come two small white kids — brothers. They're going to their home which is in this building. Their father is a policeman. They come downstairs and play whenever they can. There are six little girls out front, too.

"Say, why don't you kids go downstairs and play? The Playroom is open."

There are three other little children out here playing on the ice and I suppose that it will just be a matter of minutes before they come downstairs, too. There is a mother at the window watching some of her children playing down here. She doesn't seem to be worried about them. They're doing all right.

Usually I park my truck out here and the kids climb all over it. I worry that they'll scratch up my new paint job but that's par for the course. All part of the program.

Here come some little girls pushing doll carriages. They're heading toward the Playroom. Now there are two or three children running around with no coats or hats on. It looks like they sneaked out of the house. They're turning back in again. I hope they get in before mom gets home. School has just let out and the kids have gone home to be with their mothers and then they'll most likely come out and play.

I see a visiting nurse who is walking across the project. She seems a little lost. She has boots on and is carrying a little briefcase and a loose-leaf notebook. She's a colored girl, very young. There are always people coming into projects. The white man coming out of that building just now looks like a bill collector. I suppose he just tried to collect some insurance money or something.

Well, I think I'll go on back to the Playroom. It's cold out here and my ears are beginning to turn. Between the buildings I can see what looks like about fifty kids on sleds going down a hill. It's very icy. There are hundreds of kids around that we could get into our program but I guess sliding is a thing which is much more attractive than what we have to offer at the moment. Maybe they'll come a little later on.

Here we are back in the Playroom again. A lot more kids are trying to get in.

"You don't want these children in? Put them out?! Tell her to put them out!"

The kids are all gone now and it's the end of the day. The teen-agers are busy cleaning up the place and getting it in order. The toys have to be put away. Then it will be time for our evaluation meeting.

The meeting has just begun. Tony is having fits. He doesn't believe that we should have meetings. He comes to them all but he gets very disgusted. What seems to be the trouble, Tony?

Tony: I'll be all right.

Reed: Well, this is what makes the world go around — conversation. That's what makes the President to be the President — talking. We've got to learn to talk more.

Tony: Okay.

Belenky: Now tomorrow we're going to have some visitors from Harvard — a group of students. I'm not going to be here. It will be you teenagers and Jim. This visit means a lot because we want Harvard to keep on supporting the Playroom. Everything has to come off well. Any suggestions about what we can do with these people?

Tony: Do we have to be here until five tomorrow?

Belenky: Every day. Every day.

Gail: But I've worked my thirty-five hours this week and I want a day off. The Neighborhood Youth Corps said that it would be coming to me.

Belenky: Look. Let's settle one thing at a time. What are we going to do with these students tomorrow? I would suggest that you might take a few minutes to sit down and talk with them. Tell them what you're doing down here and what you plan to do.

Tony: So, we're going to have to sit here tomorrow morning and *talk*?!

Belenky: Yes, sir, *talk*! I also suggest that you take them on a tour of the neighborhood and show them both projects. Are you with me?

Tony: I want to be alone!

Belenky: But at the moment you are part of a group, an employee, and you have a job to do.

(Man, I *really* came on like the Man! That was the nub of the issue around which we later exploded. In reading

31

over this material I am amazed at how I sounded. But the kids got to me when they didn't function on my terms. The words themselves aren't too bad. The kids no doubt could profit from firm expectations. But the effect which I can recall was one of frustration, annoyance. I knew the kids only slightly at the time and could not presume to understand their rhythm and moods. One has to know the effects beforehand of any contemplated intervention. To do that one has to know the child. To know the child one has to make errors and so it goes. Goddam, in such work as this — people-work — one must have an enormous tolerance for ambiguity and error.)

*　*　*

December 7, 1966; Wednesday

Now I'm at an Education Department faculty meeting at Boston College and I'm noticing how *white* everyone is. Just came from the Playroom after driving the mothers to a supermarket where we bought pork chops and stuff. Mrs. Pulley cooked and we all ate delightedly amid rock and roll recorded music. Arthur Davis danced with Mrs. Searcy. How dead it is in Academia. Speech professor whose s's hiss is pleading for a faculty-sponsored witch-hunt to root out mispronouncers. "If you have a student in your class who speaks indifferently, we should *know* it." Poor fellow was nervous. The world is so unbelievably arbitrary. Why should this character have a cushy, well-paying, respected position and Mr. Johnson*, a man of *real* talent, have to settle for nothing? Johnson is black.

*　*　*

Let me tell you what we did and then if we have time I'll try to explain why we did it. . . .

(I'm sitting with my feet up on the desk and blue denims and sandals against the radio and the adding machine, and Alice, almost ten, is fussing with the light on the sofa trying to avoid homework and I'm flooded with recall, dancing around the edges of productivity tingling with excitement and fear. It all happened so long ago. Almost four years.)

* * *

October 27, 1965

Wild! Yesterday and the day before Jim Reed, Jay Clark and I rode like exotic spirits through the housing projects on our bicycles. In and out of the parking lots and basketball courts.

"Ha, ha," roared a five-year-old.

"What's so damned funny?" roared I.

"Big men on bicycles," roared he.

We were looking for somebody. One Huey Joyner. Heard he is a social worker assigned by the city to work with Negro kids on the north side of Parker Street — the black project; Mission Hill Extension. He's new to the job but grew up in the project. Mother still lives here.

We stopped people. "Where's Huey?" To perfect strangers.

Men on bicycles. Acting like kids. Must be nutty.

Jim Reed. Big, black with Zapata moustache and a beret. Has a delightfully complex, play-hostile way of asking simple questions.

Jay Clark. Collegiate, athletic, clean-cut. Bicycling is *his* bit. Catholic pacifist. Not sure he's a pacifist, come to think of it, but he kind of comes on like a Quaker.

* * *

And how did we get there? Jay and I were hired by the Harvard Graduate School of Education to work on something called the Shadow Faculty, the purpose of which, at least as some of us originally understood it, was to design and set up an urban laboratory high school. It never really worked because we argued all the time and Harvard eventually lost its generous Research and Development grant. But Jay and I got to develop an innovative urban child guidance and/or school psychology program.

We had worked together quite a bit in the past and had a pretty good idea about how the other guy went about things. Vaguely I was aware that Jay, influenced by an internship at the Judge Baker Child Guidance Center, wanted to set up some sort of community counseling service. I, still decompressing from a summer program in which we used Neighborhood Youth Corpsmen to work with local children, had a big thing about big kids working with little kids. We were in agreement that we both wanted to involve local, nonprofessional citizenry. And we both felt strongly that we needed a third member of our team — a person who was closer to kids from poor neighborhoods than we could ever be. We felt, too, that we needed a black person since we are both white and hoped to set up a program that would deal with and hopefully bring together white and black communities . . . to say nothing of universities, hospitals, suburbs, businesses, and other fantastic things.

*   *   *

First impression of Jim Reed

September 22, 1965
Highly recommended by civil-rights friends. We visited him in his Cambridge garret, second floor, rear, of a huge attic-

barn. Amid the paints, brushes, tables, half-finished pictures, half-erected plasterboard walls, books, old clothes, food, a country stove with coffee, stood Jim Reed! A bear of a man, brusque and impatient; defensive perhaps but not really unfriendly. Loquacious. Offered us some stew, some coffee. Wiped the sweat from his brow. Dramatic, tough, yet sensitive, intelligent, argumentative, determined, a sense of who he is, the power to move forward, a magnificent model for kids; very black, unashamedly himself. Kids would go immediately for a guy like this.

* * *

And I'm sitting here four years later. Jim is now working for Arthur D. Little and Jay is at B.U. and the Playroom is still going strong but needs money. We had a fund-raising party for the Playroom last Saturday. I got delightfully drunk and enjoyed it but hate being told by graduate students that I am the older generation.

Well, before meeting Jim we went to Concord Prison to look for potential co-workers. Jay had contact with the prisoner's Self-Development Group and we sat in on an interesting session. Made friends with people we later met on the outside. Didn't find staff though. Walked around Roxbury with Gail Washington, a beautiful black artist who teaches in a junior high school. False starts. Talked with Cornell Eaton (later sadly killed). On the steps of the church Eaton said that he wants the job but a better man would be Jim Reed. And that's how we met him.

> The story is henceforth one of conflict and learning confrontation, unstaged. . ... And growing respect . . . .
> There were other things, of course.
> Eating soul food at Pauline's restaurant.

Trying to hold the teen-agers together.
And the Mission Church. The poor whites.
Father Forrest.

* * *

There was a meeting of the Mission Hill poverty
group one night. They were trying to write a proposal for
the OEO agency — ABCD (Action for Boston Community
Development). It was a long meeting and now hard to
remember, but afterwards Jay and I and Val Hyman, a
black social worker from the Roxbury Associated Neighborhood Houses, went for a prolonged coffee chat with a
couple of black women from the project. We went to the
Howard Johnson's (now a parking lot near the Sunoco
station. I thought I knew a lot about blacks (Negroes in
those days). So I instructed them on being black and the
political meaning that adhered to therein or some such
thing. (I squirm at the recollection.)

September 17, 1965
Quite a discussion got going. Left at about one a.m. Came
out of it as "white liberal finks." I was arguing for the
possibility of dramatic personal change given drastic change
in the situation. "You choose to be what you are, who you
are," I said. Sounded like an accusation and they responded
to it as such. They wondered what Jay and I will get out of
this after we publish and become rich and famous by using
them as data. Such cynicism is a thin veneer, I think, although paradoxically it runs deep.
(Oh, the arrogance. . . .)

* * *

Why that neighborhood? Well, Jay and I had looked around

36

Boston for a community with visible problems such as high delinquency rates, racial tension, school failure. We wanted to be where experts like us could make a "valuable contribution." Traveled here and there around town. Spoke to a lot of people who seemed to know the city well. People at Harvard wanted us to locate in Cambridge so as to be convenient to the School of Education.

It soon became obvious that Mission Hill was just about perfect. It's a predominantly Irish Catholic section of the city but has a large and expanding minority of blacks who are packed mostly into one housing project — the "Extension" — which is directly across Parker Street from a virtually all-white project — Mission Hill proper. The projects are under one management; have one name — Mission Hill — although two rent-collection windows (white and col'ed). Oh, just you try and cross Parker Street the wrong way on a warm dark night. An old black lady was beaten recently, they told us. But once it was even worse.

People who know say Mission is the second-worst project in the city — next to Columbia Point. Columbia Point is worse because it is an island in the midst of nothing, no stores, no services, nothing. Human Misery a function of half-witted planning.

We chose Mission because the possibilities seemed so much greater than Columbia Point. There was a nonproject city all around. Up on the Hill were middle-class Irish homeowners, for example. Then there were resources. Virtually all of Harvard Medical School, Children's Hospital, Boston Lying-In, Peter Bent Brigham, The Boston Fine Arts Museum, the Boston Conservatory, several excellent colleges — including Wheelock with whom we later developed a fine working relationship. And parks, theaters, public transportation, stores, everything.

But all of this was now irrelevant to the functioning of the community (or communities). In fact Harvard — the

37

Medical School — appeared as the sworn enemy of the whites, the Irish Catholics.

Mission Church was the focus of a once vibrant community. The church was built by Irish stonecutters who had escaped from the nineteenth century potato famine. Hewn by hand from the rocks of the hill, it became a basilica, the leading Catholic church in New England. It still puts on a passion play every Easter, and on Sundays and holidays cars from the suburbs and even other states clog the streets and the project's parking lots and well-dressed people participate in the ceremonies. (A Greek Orthodox Church is nearby and the same is true — vestiges.)

But Harvard needed to expand and, so with the collaboration of the Boston Redevelopment Authority (BRA), it began to take over buildings by purchase and eminent domain. Father Kelley, the Mission Church rector, and his assistant, the magnificently indigenous Father McDonough, led the picket line to city hall and stopped them for a while. But their organization (MUNIT), reflecting the community, was also antiblack and saw a Harvard, BRA, black conspiracy . . . .

The black project seemed worn, depressed; poor facilities compared to the white: a dingy basement for meetings compared to a large, finished recreation hall; high-rise buildings with elevators often not working, broken windows, piss smell in the hallways, a broken-down basketball court, stark, asphalt, factory-like. The whites had all low-rise buildings, some landscaping, a better but still inadequate recreation area . . . . It's bad all over, but these distinctions make a difference. "How come you're working with the niggers? Everybody does things for *them!* Why don't they do something for themselves for a change?"

Except for a struggling ladies-run Mission Hill Extension Civic Association and a boys' club Huey Joyner had recently formed, there was no visible organization, and a psycho-

logical separation from central Roxbury, where civil
rights and service groups were becoming active.

We decided to work with whites, blacks, and Harvard.

* * *

In the interest of clarity perhaps now we'd better focus in on
the Shadow Faculty for a bit because Harvard was important
in all of what follows, if for no other reason than its infinite
monetary- and time-consuming capacities.

"What is the Shadow Faculty? It may best be thought of
as characters in search of an author — a number of professional educators, brought together because of common
concerns, who are searching for a meaningful way of struc-
turing their existence." (From a Shadow Faculty memorandum, September 1968.)

Don Oliver has stated:

> I do not think it is the role of the university-
> centered school of education to "tinker." Let
> one major private university have the courage to
> start from the beginning, ask deep and searching
> questions about purposes, and then have the gall
> to construct viable models and explore the
> consequences through systematic research.

And when Jim Reed attended his first meeting, he commented:

> As a Negro and not a university man I was dis-
> turbed and at a loss to determine just what comes
> under the jurisdiction of education in their think-
> ing. When they say, "We want to redesign American
> Education," where does the line of demarcation
> come between such words and the doing, the
> actual doing? So I sit there and I'm filled with all
> kinds of emotions. On the one hand I know how
> the Negro is crying for education, how badly he
> needs it, and on the other hand I know I'm look-

39

ing at some great minds. I am in the presence of
genius. But I would hate like the devil to get up
and try to convince them of anything. The way they
jump on each little word. Rhetoric plays a
dominant role in their conversation. I suppose
that's as it should be because that's the medium
through which they impart their ideas. This is one
of their tools and it has to be used effectively.
But I sit there and I feel terribly frightened for
the Negro community. I feel that these are the
people who *can* do something about the condition
that the Negro is in and they don't give a damn to
try. Like they see there's a guy out swimming and
he gets in trouble and starts to drown. They stand
there and say: "I'm not the lifeguard. My job is to
determine how strong the current is and if there
are sharks. In fact, I *need* you to drown for me so I
can accurately assess the dangers, you see." They
talked of revolutions yesterday at the Shadow
Faculty and they don't even have my name in the
directory as the guy who carries the coffee.

* * *

September 22, 1965

When we talked with Jim he wanted to know the details of
our operation; what exactly it was that we wanted to do;
what his role would be. We told him frankly that we had very
little clearly planned, but many ideas, inclinations, possibilities, and that we wanted to play it as we went, working
collaboratively, developing something that would eventually
make sense for the community as well as Harvard. He wanted
to know what Harvard stood to gain, what they wanted. We
explained the vagaries of the Shadow Faculty. We told him
that, as for us, we wanted to set up a model guidance program

for high school kids that would involve having them do something for themselves and others rather than having their psyches explored. We told Jim that we felt that current secondary school guidance as we understood it — especially when it came to head-shrinking — was irrelevant and inefficient. If only there could be a working together of school and community. . . .

October 27, 1965
Cold October day. Shirt and tie for Jay. No jacket. Peddles his bike smoothly. Fast. Old machine but goes well. Mine is new but the seat is stuck — won't go up or down. A symbol?

Memorandum

October 11, 1965
To: Dean Sizer, Henry Olds, John Herzog
From: Bob Belenky and Jay Clark
    This is to bring you up to date on our thinking with regard to the child guidance subproject of the Shadow Faculty which we have decided to call Psycho-Educational Action Research, henceforth to be affectionately known as PEAR. We have two major objectives: The first is to develop a viable model for those guidance counselors, school psychologists, school social workers, and other mental health practitioners who work in urban schools. We feel that neither personal-problem counseling nor training in decision-making skills are in themselves adequate approaches to meet the monumental problems that exist today. Delinquency and milder forms of antisocial behavior — including marginal commitment to the purpose of the school — reflect in children, we suspect, the greater alienation of the larger community from a variety of social institutions, including the school.
    We intend to deal with guidance problems on a social-

41

psychological rather than on an intrapsychic level. Our client in a sense will not be the referred child alone but the entire child-family-school-community complex. This we hope to accomplish by involving the community in activities which speak to its most salient needs while at the same time encouraging it to draw upon existing learning resources in and around the city.

Research, at least of an evaluative sort, will be built in eventually.

* * *

There was then the problem of where we were going to locate. We needed an office, an apartment or a storefront to carry on our enterprise. We petitioned Harvard for rent money but met with reluctance unless we could tell them exactly *why* we needed a place. This, of course we couldn't do. Meanwhile we made friends with the young, courageous Father Forrest of Mission Church who offered to let us use an office in one of the church-owned buildings despite our Harvard sponsorship and black affiliations.

October 28, 1965
We're not there yet but we're moving along!

Getting an apartment within the housing project didn't work out because Harvard wasn't about to cough up the rent money. It's just as well. Our present location is ideal. We're in a huge church-owned building, St. Alphonsus's Hall. It's right in the heart of white territory but not far from Negro turf. Elegant facilities. Huge offices. Marble fireplaces. Under-used recreational facilities; six bowling alleys, gym, theater-type auditorium, jukebox, etc. Negroes, however, are not welcome because they "don't live in the parish." The parish line, by the merest coincidence, is Parker Street, the very same street that separates the whites from the blacks. Well, maybe we can change all that. Certainly can't have our program without Negroes. Father Forrest would like to involve blacks in his program and feels that Jim Reed's charisma will help make that possible . . . along maybe with our program money.

Damn, but we need kids! Don't know what we'll do with them, though; but once they're around, I'm certain a purpose will occur to us. I still like the idea of big kids working with little kids.

This afternoon Jim, Jay, and I wandered around the two projects equipped with tape recorder, cameras, football, and high spirits. To meet kids. Ambling along sticking microphones in people's faces, shooting pictures, saying silly things. Kid said he liked living in Maine better than here and another one wanted to be a queen for Halloween and have slaves and another kid had a brown dog and they followed us everywhere. Jay told that dumb story about the elephant hunt. They loved it. Then back to the white project and St. Alphonsus's and the Negro kids wanted to follow us but they dropped off soon after we crossed Parker Street.

There were more Negro kids in the white project than I had expected.

"Help me get my feet back on the ground," sang one kid.

Jay thinks this is a plea. Lots of kids here seem so much in need of something. One boy with such bitten nails and the little girl peering at Jay from behind the building when he told the dumb elephant story, afraid to approach. Then she told Jim that she wanted him to take her brother's picture. He obliged by taking *her* picture.

It's fun doing just what we're doing. It's nice to be around kids for a change.

* * *

October 31, 1965

Jim Reed and his new wife, Joyce, were at the PEAR office today unloading a filing cabinet and other equipment which

43

Jim decided to bring over in his truck. Seemed kind of unnecessary to me. The store said they would deliver it on Tuesday. Guess he likes to have some use for his truck. It's big and powerful like him.

Jay bicycles in. He suggests that we go find some project kids and get to know them. We wander around. Jay carries the football which we've decorated with silly pictures. Meet some kids and toss the ball around with them. Get involved in many games and conversations with kids along the way.

Discovered a man in a car near the entrance of the Mission Hill Civic Association meeting room. Explained that he was from some kind of city recreation office and that in honor of Halloween he was about to show cartoon-type movies to the local children. But he needed a key. We found Huey Joyner, who found a key. Jay and I invited all the kids in. As the man set up the projector we led the kids in singing. All the kids were Negro. Jay got the bright idea to round up some whites. Came back in five minutes with maybe fifteen. Nothing to this integration thing, really.

Some tension in the air today between Jim and myself. Why?

* * *

November 1, 1965; Jim Reed

When white people get intimate with me in conversation they eventually infer something about their ancestry. It may be ever so slight. "Well, my grandfather did so and so, and so did my *great* grandfather. . . ." We Negroes feel that we've got to have some identity, too. Who the hell are we? Every once in a while an art book will come out in which they'll show architecture down in New Orleans. Negro slaves who had a knowledge of ironwork in Africa were brought here as slaves. Many of the wrought-iron designs that one sees in the South are African.

44

The point is that there are many, many things which point to the fact that the Negro didn't just come up out of the ground. He had a history. But he doesn't have great volumes to *prove* his history. So people say, "Well, he is nothing; a savage." Negro children growing up today need to know the history of their people so they'll have something on which to build. Without it they're lost.

So what's this bringing on? Schools, schools, schools and more schools — all over America. The Black Arts in New York; Freedom Library in Philadelphia; organizations that have been running tutorial programs are now starting their own schools. Books are being printed. And the alphabet . . . A is for Africa, K is for King, M is for Malcolm . . .

So when one starts to talk about how they can deal with inner city education and they exclude this thinking and action within the Negro community, I wonder how effective their program is likely to be. There is a *revolution* going on. The warriors are girding their loins and the din of battle is going to be heard much more loudly in the months to come.

* * *

November 2, 1965

The discussion with Jim was a most productive one. I think the air got cleared, and hopefully trust was reestablished. Jim seemed to take a strong Negro nationalist position and I seemed to be left holding a flimsy integrationist bag.

I think we're ready to move ahead now. We have a number of things planned and I think we could carry off any that we choose. All are potentially exciting. Jim's Negro history idea seems certain to capture the interest and imagination of parents if not children. At the same time my thought of working at least at first as a kind of *ad hoc* school psychology department for the Mission High (Catholic) seems like a pretty good way of involving ourselves with the white community. Finally, if we could make contact with the state's reform school administration (The Youth Service Board), we could design a program to help released delinquents reenter their community.

* * *

Last night I was used as a psychologist around here for the first time. Father Forrest asked about a nineteen-year-old boy (white; Italian extraction) whom he was about to accompany to a state hospital. Kid was involved in terrible happenings. He and a friend had attempted to mug a guy. The guy had a gun and killed the friend. The kid ran away in a panic. Has a long history of defeat, anger, loss. Father, whom he hated, died two years ago. Thrown out of kindergarten at age five. Teacher told mother at the time that in her thirty years of experience she had never seen such a troublesome (not "troubled"?) child. Seemed to me frightened, angry, confused. Maybe sort of schizie.

I came along to the hospital with Forrest, the kid and his mother.

Lots of bureaucracy at the hospital. Couldn't even get simple directions to the admissions entrance. Had a long, inhospitable wait. Finally saw the doctor. Perfunctorily polite, cold, efficient, insensitive. Told the mother that the boy's problem was that he had "wrong" values and couldn't tell right from otherwise (said with stethoscope hanging from his pocket). Indicated that a stay in the hospital would cure him. Mother was impressed but in the car going home wondered how he had learned so much about her son in such a brief interview. (Kid was frisked by a bright, courteous attendant and his suitcase was searched for weapons.) I told him to look us up when he gets out. He said he would.

November 3, 1965
Jim and I went to the Boston Public Library yesterday.

46

Got library cards and film catalogs. We're thinking of showing educational films to the community every Saturday at our headquarters. Use it as a takeoff point for all sorts of things.

* * *

November 4, 1965

Jay and I wandered around the neighborhood. Ambled along to another housing project sort of down the street — Bromley-Heath. It looks like the name. Massive, desolate, endless. But in several ways better than Mission Hill. They have, for example, a playing field for teen-agers and a small but decent playground for the little kids.

We talked with a janitor about the population. Informed us sadly that a "new class" of people were moving in (capitalist? proletariat? criminal? white? black? rich? poor?) Said that neighborhood morale is on the wane and assault, battery, destruction of property and general slovenliness are on the rise. As if to prove his point, he led us into a dark basement and opened a door. There, bizarrely, and as if precisely to belie his dour report, was a lively and well-equipped nursery school.

Met the director, an aristocratic Southern Negro lady. School sponsored by Red Feather. Hours: eight to five. Especially designed for working mothers. Hot-lunch programs. Considerable work with families. Introduced the social worker. Young, Oriental, lovely.

The kids were well cared for. Basement space well used. We ought to get the Mission Hill people tuned in on this sort of thing.

Walked back to the Mission area. Dropped in on Father Forrest. Tried some of our current program thoughts out on him. Generally he liked them but felt that we were too unfocused and were biting off more than we could chew. Thought we ought to start with six- to twelve-year-olds and maybe draw in their older siblings if we still wanted to get a

47

big kids' training program going at that point. Not bad. Relatively easy to start with middle-aged kids. The danger is that we may get stuck running a simpleminded recreation program with little or no research or innovation potential.

Here is the lineup of opinion within our little group at the moment:

1. Jay thinks that all we need to do is hang around, get to know people gradually and draw them in for whatever they want when they're ready.
2. Jim is most interested in the "identity as a Negro" issue. Wants us to recruit on a door to door basis and is far more interested in adults than teen-agers or little kids.
3. I want to *get started,* am impatient with Jay's tolerance of ambiguity and, unlike Jim, want to work with kids, teen-agers; *whites* as well as Negroes.

Tomorrow Jim plans to bring in a number of Negro mothers to help us figure things out at our now traditional morning obsession session.

* * *

November 5, 1965

Hoo boy! What a meeting! Jim brought along not merely about ten mothers but one father and Sara-Ann Shaw, an articulate "movement" person. Jim, we discovered, had contacted over seventy families. Just about had our first mass meeting.

Jim chaired, introduced Jay and myself, and we each gave a monologue. Jay told of our visit to Bromley-Heath's pre-school center. Parents seemed interested.

I put in a pitch for rehabilitating teen-age delinquents. Jim said little.

Then Mrs. Shaw spoke. Had a strident, angry quality. Wanted all-black schools and all-black staff. Certainly a put-down for Jay and myself, but who knows? Maybe she's right. On the other hand, it sounds disturbingly like what they already have in the South.

A. Why deprive white kids of an opportunity to learn Negro history?

B. Mission Hill is a Negro *and* white housing project, our group is integrated and Harvard is pretty damned white. Neither Jay, I, nor Harvard seem up to playing black nationalist, but if Jim or Mrs. Shaw want to, that's their business.

Maybe while Jim does his bit, Jay and I could do something parallel and sensible with the whites and maybe gradually grow together — Irish history for the Irish, Italian history for the Italians, American history for everybody.

Jay's reaction to Mrs. Shaw was etched visibly in his face. Jim read Jay and got silently mad at him for being so predictably and wholeheartedly white. God knows what he thought of me.

Jim and I took Mrs. Shaw to lunch at a homey little Negro restaurant. Mrs. Shaw told me that I talked too much at the meeting — just like all whites — and had the effect of inhibiting the Negro audience. If not for me, she insisted, they would have supported her position. Jim agreed. I disagreed. Jim said that he'll take the tape recorder to the next all-black meeting he's at and document his thesis that Negroes in general support the separatist position — which I maintain is a moral and political disaster.

Well, then Jim and I went to see Noel Day, settlement-house director and prominent Negro intellectual. Was very busy so we had only a few minutes to talk. Put the separatist stuff in perspective. Noel pointed out that many Negroes are terribly shy with whites and, because of a history of intense oppression, are often defensively acquiescent. An all-Negro program might provide an atmosphere in which people can test themselves, develop self-confidence.

* * *

49

(This year in the fall when I begin the new job in that neighborhood as community mental health worker I think it will go better. There will be coherence, common sense, respect, and a lack of arrogance. Arrogance is hard to erase. How many thousands of sorties against peasants in the fields shaking their fists gored and bloodied. I will not cause that! How hateful to live in such a cruel country! But who *made* us wear the jackboots? Who cares? Why can't we just remove them? Here I am and there I may be in the fall. I shall wear sandals, tennis shoes. A beard. And I shall love. Life-enhancingly. Without seduction. Without reciprocation. Without guilt. I shall simply give when needed and not give when not needed. I shall simply be.)

* * *

November 7, 1965; Morning.
We argued.

We fought over Jim's request that we get him a little plastic card with his picture on it saying that he is a staff member at Harvard. Such pictures do not exist. Jim says that we must *make* them exist or he will quit. If he were a faculty member he could *have* a plastic card in red — without a picture — but Jim is *not eligible* to be a faculty member. He is a *staff* member. And staff members do not get cards. Maybe it's discriminatory but I don't see it that way. I just don't see Jim qualifying as a faculty member in the eyes of the Harvard Corporation. We even got some flack getting him on board as a staff member. He's making a mountain out of a molehill.

We also talked about Negro history courses and segregated schools.

Jay expressed considerable upset with Mrs. Shaw and told Jim that he should have checked with us before asking seventy people to come to what was essentially an executive meeting.

50

Jim was hurt and expressed his feeling that everything *he* thinks of and tries to do is wrong with us.

The whole issue is really that of identity and at least on two levels — Negro identity in general and Jim's identity as a Harvard employee. Jim is convinced that neither we nor Harvard nor indeed anyone in the white world is about to treat him as a full partner in this or any endeavor.

I think that Jim misperceives things and then sets himself up to confirm his conviction that he is getting screwed. He, on the other hand, feels that *I* misperceive things and set *him* up to get screwed.

Nevertheless I remain convinced that a decent working relationship will develop between us. If the three of us can't make it together, there would seem little hope for society at large, of which we are but an infinitesimal part.

* * *

November 7, 1965; Afternoon.
Jim and I saw a mother who has a difficult son. Negro. Spoke with the mother for a while. Boy got "impossible" five years ago when father and mother broke up. We spoke with the boy . . . really Jim did. A beautiful interviewing job. He *really* knows how to communicate with people.

Jim asked the boy what we could do for him. Kid looked uncomfortable. "You can help me find my father," he blurted.

As we were leaving, he asked Jim what size shoe he wears. "Fourteen," Jim admitted. (Almost big enough to fill.)

(Years ago a blind student was pestered every day by a kindly old lady who pitied him and wanted to be of use. "You really want to do something for me?" he asked.

"Yes indeed," she replied. "Tell me what to do."

He reached up and removed his two glass eyes, held them for her to see and said, "Make these work!")

* * *
51

November 8, 1965; Late Afternoon.
Jay and his current girl friend and I wandered around the
Extension. Jay carrying the football. Lots of kids know us
already. Jay is best known. They seem to come out from
everywhere to play with him. He has a nice manner. Some-
what controlling but wholesome, likeable, and accepting.

Went to Mrs. Ruth Spriggs' apartment to discuss plans with
her. She's the chairman of the Mission Hill Extension Civic
Association. Jay and I want to get something off the ground
now. We feel that as long as we have nothing going, the three
of us (Jim, Jay, and I) are doomed to squabble forever. With
a project we'll at least have concrete big issues to fight about.
Maybe Mrs. Spriggs can help us.

We talked with her about the possibility of using the huge
room in the basement behind the Civic Association meeting
room at 81 Prentiss Street. And just settle into it. Remove
ourselves from the marble palace at St. Alphonsus's hall and
get where the people are. At St. Alphonsus you can't leave
the door open. The janitor has to let visitors in. It's too formal. And so far no blacks have wandered over. It's distinctly
and absolutely white turf.

Here we could gradually and informally develop a program
by being there all the time. We could let kids come in to play
in the afternoon and somehow involve the adults. Child care
facilities are a very real neighborhood need.

Would mean working the Negro side of the project,
however. But how do you choose? Wherever you locate you
are on *some*body's turf. Besides the blacks seem most obviously receptive. People are friendly, open, and willing to
go along with useful ideas. Whites so far seem a bit more
suspicious, guarded, cautious. Well, the basement of 81 is
near the white project — right across Parker Street — and a
child care program lends itself to relatively easy integration.
We would try to attract *people,* regardless of color.

I mentioned a germ of this idea to Jim the other day. He

52

seemed to buy it, despite his primary interest in working with black men.

Well, Mrs. Spriggs liked the idea very much. She'll bring it up to her Civic Association at the meeting Monday night. If they approve, we may have something off the ground by Tuesday.

Hooray!

* * *

(We are always alone. I was alone then and did not know it. Alone, yet we survive. . . . The Playroom began as a dance. A quadrille. The people moved forward and back and around formally in time to music that came from elsewhere. . . . As I look out the window I see how green the yard has become. And the white gray-shadowed deep snow of the winter seems just to have passed, but I still feel a chill and have to keep the windows shut; perhaps it will warm up later. I am alone and the music from the radio on the shelf above my desk is formal.)

* * *

Oh, I don't know how to go on with this.

Things got confusing and mixed up. There was a lot of stewing around for a while. We saw a lot of people and gave speeches. And then there were those endless airy arguments at the Shadow Faculty. Jim and I seemed to get along better. We went to that Civic Association Meeting and told them about our plan to run an activity program in the project but said that *they* must lead. We would serve primarily as instigators and resource people. We would share our formal learning with them, just as their work would help us in our research, whatever that was, and so on. They liked what they heard and we had approval and we called another meeting.

53

Then there was the "Great Eastern Blackout." And my family was angry with me because I was never around.

* * *

November 11, 1965

We had the Great Eastern Blackout, a monument to fail-safe thinking. Got home by car and wanted to listen to the transistor radio but Mike and Alice were involved in some silly business and I couldn't hear. I roared a threat of a whack apiece on the behind. Before bedtime I yelped at them again for nothing in particular. Mike cried and told Mary: "Daddy only comes home to eat supper and scream at us." In the morning Mary yelled at me for not picking up my socks. Accused: "You only come home to eat supper and scream at us." I *used* to carry out the garbage, she said, but don't even do that any more. Sheepishly I carried out the garbage and left, mumbling something about a teen-age dance that night which would mean that as far as supper was concerned. . . . There are so many conflicting demands. The program is enjoyable and involving but I can't make a mess of everything else. Must work things out. Try efficiency. Plan my time.

Consulted with the Mission High School. Saw four boys, mostly underachieving. Talked with the principal, Sister Coena. Bright, no-nonsense, pleasant woman. Lunch meeting with the Mission Hill Interagency Council. Medical students want to serve the poor community. No lunch. Long conversation with fellow from the white project. Works for the housing authority. Complained that Negroes get all the services and they ought to "do something for themselves." Had a fine party for the Neighborhood Youth Corps kids who worked with us last summer. Gail and Tony would like to work with us again.

November 12, 1965

We had a meeting with the Extension mothers today. Only three came. The activists. Meeting called to implement our suggestion that a children's program get set up. Bogged down in all sorts of details such as: What time shall it be held? Should we have an on-the-job training program or a preliminary orientation period, or both? How can we recruit more people? The details unnerved me. If Jay, Jim, and I just took the bull by the horns and *began* the damned program (*any* damned program), we'd all be better off. The democratic process is tedious. What if we just moved into 81. Practical. And put in a telephone, a filing cabinet, and a lock and just stayed there all day every day, drinking coffee and fooling around. Little kids and grown-ups would sooner or later wander in out of curiosity if nothing else. There would be bull sessions and sandwiches and coffee . . . lots of coffee . . . and the little kids would play quiet games while the adults would sort of interact with each other and with the kids. And we would pursue our elegant scholarly pursuits. Now *there's* a program for you! Calculated chaos. No schedules. No dragging people in. Or throwing them out. *Screw* organization!

Spoke with a white mother today after lunch. "Why *not* bring my child over to the Extension for a good, supervised program?" she said. "We don't mind Negroes." She said she couldn't speak for the other mothers but she imagined that many of them would feel as she does. "Unsupervised kids hanging around all the time are a *big* problem and even the many organized activities in the white Project do not meet the need." Her own four-year-old has nothing to do and no one to play with.

November 16, 1965

Met with a few mothers in the morning. Only four people

55

came but that's one better than last time. A beautiful, very dark lady whose name I've forgotten agreed to get a schedule filled in with at least two names of mothers to help out each morning and two each afternoon. Probably the program will run only in the morning for a while. Jay thinks we ought to start out small, maybe a day or two a week, and gradually expand. I want to keep it open all the time. Jay is right in that we shouldn't overextend ourselves but I feel that we'll make it much better with this community and have a better program in the long run if we are informal, warm, homey and eminently available.

* * *

Talked with Mrs. Spriggs about getting proposals in shape for tonight's poverty program meeting. The Extension might even come out of it with money to hire mothers to run this basement program if the ladies play their cards right. Mrs. Spriggs has some neat ideas about a day care center and a summer camp.

I then went to a Shadow Faculty meeting — too many words. The aristocratic aimlessness of it all got to me.

Back to Mission Hill to see Mrs. Spriggs about proposal writing.

We cleaned up the room, some kids wandered in, and that was it; that's how the program was begun. And god said let there be a recreation program and there was. Mrs. Mary Morris, a white woman who lives in the Extension, came with her son. Just sort of wandered in and stayed to help. That was how we got integrated. Then Gail Titus, one of the Neighborhood Youth Corps kids from last summer, dropped in and found some useful things to do. Thus our teen-age program was begun.

More kids came — about fifteen, mostly black. We thought it would be nice to have more whites so Jim and I went to

Mission proper and tossed a football around. Women stuck their heads out of windows and we told them about our program, how we wanted kids to come to the basement club room and how we wanted mothers to pitch in and help make it work. Everyone we talked with felt that it was a great idea. They said they would be delighted to send their kids and would be more than happy to lend a hand . . . unfortunately we didn't take names.

We returned to the basement with about ten white kids and one brown puppy; told the owner that we don't allow animals on leashes so the beastie was turned loose and ran all over the place charming about half the kids and scaring the other half.

Jim talked with some of the older white boys — eleven-, twelve-year-olds — about a dance they wanted to run. Then he played checkers with them. They love him. The rest of the kids drew with crayons and made things with glue and paper. Quiet and businesslike — especially after the puppy peed on the floor. We told the kids it was time to go. And they went. And there wasn't even any trouble getting rid of them.

(Today I went back to the neighborhood and met with the people on the new job with the Mass. Mental Health Center. Community Mental Health. An adjacent neighborhood. Jamaica Plain. Almost five years later. No, three and a half years. What difference does it make? Four five six three years? Time goes by quickly. It was a glorious sunny coolish cloudless early June Monday and I was in love with everything. The very opposite of Weltschmerz. Drifted up the chartered streets and inquired directions to the Hillside House, which is a group home for delinquent boys I had visited years ago when they were first getting started. Rang the bell and no one answered so I went upstairs and knocked. Mrs. Hays, young, attractive, came to the door, invited me in and we talked about what it's about. I was impressed but oddly distracted by the warm grace with which the little girl fondled her mother's arm.

57

Went swimming and came to the backyard to write.

The gray wooden picket fence and the leaves making light on the black pear tree.

Obscenely elegant. I love trees, mountains, and oceans and swimming, skiing, and visual beauty in the conventional sense.

Of what use can I possibly be to the poor?

Any approach, request or correction is an intrusion and often unkind because it jolts the other out of the protective fantasies he has woven around him.

A woman may be attractive if she thinks so. If she doesn't it may be for good reason. Perhaps fear; maybe paradoxically a challenge, a dare, a threat. If one sees her beauty and tells her, what then? Harmless or even kind in intent, it may be sadly unfair because it does not respect the silence that was overtly requested, the simplicity that was adaptive.

Perhaps the same principle applies to communities. Maybe it's best to respond to the explicit message. On the other hand there may be times when seduction is right and therapeutic.

God! There may *never* be satisfaction! To play this well one has to transcend morality and *listen* not only to them but to one's *self.*

The rub of course is that then there will never be justice, only an endless scramble after unshared, unripened, and therefore empty delight. None of us knows what we want or what we're doing. Half the time we grope for the other and half the time we masturbate.

* * *

November 18, 1965

Jim Reed lectured to my Harvard MAT tutorial students. He dropped in just as we were discussing Negro families. Somebody asked him a question and he went on for about an hour and a half in reply. When he ran out of wind, somebody else threw him a question and on he went for another half hour.

It was about himself, growing up, going to school, deciding on a career. The Klan murdered his father, his mother died soon afterwards. He was very young then. He was brought up in homes and orphanages. The students were spellbound. Jim sensed this and was spurred on. He was profound, yet witty; personal, yet universal. There was something of Mark Twain in his humor. I feel a new respect and closeness to Jim. His life is a work of passionate art.

In the morning I wandered down to our new basement headquarters. Jay was there and so was Gail Titus. Jack Carter*, a teen-age kid recently thrown out of elementary school, was there, too. Referred by the courts. Totally illiterate. Withdrawn. Jim wasn't around at first but then showed up looking sick. He wanted to stay around though. Mrs. Jamesetta Sheerer was at the typewriter, preparing the stencil for the Civic Association Newsletter, a monthly of which she is the editor. Mrs. Morris, soft-spoken, polite, came in with two of her kids. The kids played with toys.

Jay felt that we needed a staff meeting. So we all sat down and talked. It was agreed that formal training for the parents and teens is essential but there was concern lest anything too formal drive away the very people we want to reach. We decided that we would encourage parents to arrive at ten o'clock in the morning and spend perhaps a half hour making plans for the day. The major emphasis would be on doing, not on talking. Research may be brought in but only if it fits. We agreed that we would have our first training session on Friday.

Later more women wandered in. One, a great-grandmother, Mrs. Ames, a profoundly elegant Negro lady. Tiny Mrs. Harding came in, too. Some of us sat and talked informally about nothing in particular and others played with the children. Gail was very helpful. Quietly kept things on an even keel. More kids wandered in. The ladies got into a discussion about what's wrong with men in the project. Very few seem to be living with their families. Huge problem for both the white and Negro groups. Women angry but half expect it. "Men are like that. They think it's their right." But what about Mr. F., I asked? *He* lives at home. I see him taking walks with his kids. Appears to love his wife. "That *really* is a man," Mrs. Harding said.

Mrs. Harding thinks men lack religion. Mrs. Morris thinks they lack jobs, *good* jobs, with masculine dignity. We talked about the service professions — teaching, social work, psychiatry, recreation and about openings and the Byzantine preconditions. Discussed therapy for the individual versus social change and social action as strategies in demythification. Some of us psychologists are moving away from individual psychotherapy, I explained, becoming intense and hopelessly longwinded. Mrs. Harding left.

Then Mrs. Barbara Searcy came in. Pleasant, energetic woman. Surrounded by several kids. Heard about the program and wanted to sign up. Didn't know some of the other women; was introduced. We talked and explained our plans. Put her in charge of calling up all the mothers who have thus far shown interest and telling them about the plans for the next few days. The meeting ended on a note of general excitement and enthusiasm. This whole thing is exciting. I feel like a Wright brother.

November 20, 1965
Yesterday morning eight mothers showed up for the training session on reading stories to children. I felt uneasy about attempting to teach experienced mothers anything at all about children. But they assured me that, while they felt competent with their own kids, the prospect of being put in a teacherlike role with other people's children worried them and they would therefore appreciate any advice or support. Jim was there too and characteristically not at

all shy about making contributions. Jay rolled in on his bike after a while and proceeded to verbalize generously.

We had a pile of children's books. I asked the mothers to spend five minutes or so observing some of the preschoolers in order to decide somehow which of the books stood the best chance of holding their interest most effectively. Each watched the kids and then picked her book and justified her choice to the rest of the group. The ladies then took turns reading their story aloud to the adults now role-playing preschoolers. Jim cried for his mommy and Jay said he was afraid to go to school because the teacher hits his brother on the knuckles with a rattan. The ladies did not hesitate to shut these boys up but sadly did not attempt to deal with the issues they raised.

Finally, they read to the group of real preschoolers. There was some discussion afterwards. The women critiqued each other politely but accurately. Struck me that Mrs. Searcy and Mrs. Reese do about as well in this reading business as most seasoned kindergarten teachers and certainly better than the green ones.

Jim, Jay, Gail, and I went out for lunch. Red-tape problems with the Neighborhood Youth Corps leave us in doubt about Gail's salary. We've called each day and get assurances but still no check. So we treat her to lunch occasionally and lend her carfare. So far she's been remarkably patient.

After lunch we went to speak with the project manager, Mr. Sullivan. A hearty colonial, he gets mad at Negroes for the destruction of *his* housing project "after all we've done for them." Wow. Well, if he can't see the revolution in a busted elevator, so much the worse for him and the rest of us.

Jim and Jay went around Mission proper (the white area) with the football to recruit and canvass the whites. I went back to the basement to see how things were going. Going?

Holy cow, Batman, they were *gone*! Seventy kids — give or take fifteen. Looked like a hundred and seventy. Three mothers and Gail were keeping watch but the task was clearly impossible.

Oddly, however, total chaos did not prevail. Most of the kids were more or less quietly painting and coloring. It's just that there were so many of them, it *looked* incredibly wild. Then Mrs. Sheerer organized a very energetic musical chairs game in the middle of the floor which, while usefully channeling overexuberance, tended to create and stabilize an extremely high noise level. Added to this was the contrapuntal shrieking of four or five little ones who did nothing but run back and forth the length of the basement.

I grabbed a book, sat down in the middle of the floor, and read a story to the gang. Most of them were six and seven-ish so I tried *Lassie*, then *The Three Little Pigs,* which aroused far more interest, given the noisy circumstances. Lots of little kids around me, sitting as close as they could; on my lap, around and all over me. We tried *Captain Small*. The kids read along with me, those old enough to know how.

Mrs. Sheerer did what seemed suicidal to me at the time; she promoted a goddamned relay race! Although she's a competent organizer, I felt that a much calmer tone should have been set. I didn't know how to communicate this without hurting her feelings. So I let it pass. She managed.

Jay came in to report that he and Jim did well with the canvassing. Many white mothers expressed an interest and a willingness to work.

We called "time" on the kids. Told them to put things away and clean up. Lots of horseplay but the job got done. It was Mrs. Sheerer again who organized it. Clearly either she or Mrs. Searcy should be the head teacher-mother.

We gave the children who helped a cookie apiece as a reward. Everyone left except Gail, myself, and a bunch of noisy ten-year-oldish boys who absolutely refused to leave. Finally got rid of them, except for two who hid provocatively. I told them to come into the other room and TALK WITH ME! Sounded like a principal. The boys were terrified. One escaped but I grabbed the other and with Gail's help brought him into the other room where, scared out of his wits but high as a kite, he promised to leave on time in the future. But when he got out of my grasp he ran victoriously out of the door, defiant, hostile, and frantic. I can see how teachers get into bad things with kids. Hard to be nice.

* * *

Perhaps now is the time to step back a bit and look over what has been accomplished. Three guys swoop into a neighborhood and, equipped with boyish charm and a football, rush about and eventually get a project off the ground which, although studiously devoid of scientific underpinnings, seems to have met a community need, to have aroused the interest and commitment of local citizens, and to have offered some promise for long-term success and growth. Naturally one would expect ups and downs in the road ahead, but at least the basic groundwork for a worthwhile project seems to have been laid without backbreaking labor or painful disappointments. In retrospect the impression of cavalier early success is confirmed. While complex problems eventually arose, in the beginning all that seemed required was enthusiasm, time, and good will.

December 4, 1965
Sitting in front of the fireplace in New Hampshire. The days move on so quickly. The program is getting bigger and is already a bit out of hand. Have we bitten off more than we can chew?

On Wednesday Jim and I presented an exciting version

of our acitivities to Dave McClelland's seminar for his junior faculty lieutenants. We were inspirational but tended to lie.

I don't know. They were hardly big, overt lies. They were harmless, barely noticeable ones. It's hard for us, involved in the project, to distinguish clearly between what *really* happened, and what we wanted to happen, and what we had merely hoped would happen or had planned to have happen in the very near future. We're a good vaudeville team, Jim and I. And probably exaggerate no more than most people who talk about what they are engrossed in.

We've arranged to have the Neighborhood Youth Corps pay a small salary to our teen-age aides and are negotiating with something called "the Commonwealth Service Corps" to pay the mothers a stipend. This latter organization was originally designed to attract student-type volunteers to work *with* the poor, but now it's trying to attract the poor as well. It offers eighty dollars a month, which is okay for a student who wants to make a sacrifice but for a mother or father with a family it is simply a dreadfully substandard wage. However, since the eighty dollars will not be deducted from welfare payments as other income is, the deal is perhaps slightly less than obscene.

I watched the teen-agers work with little kids on Thursday afternoon and for part of Friday. They did well but tended to blow up when the little kids wouldn't obey them. We have to discuss control techniques.

Thursday we had an evaluation session after the little kids left, and on Friday we had a fifteen-minute premeeting and a short postsession. These meetings are good. Some of the teen-agers (we now have six) seem to be very reluctant to accept structure and planning and seem quite unable to attempt a balanced critique of their own efforts. I get the feeling that they are too absolute about things as well as generally negative. They are too ready to damn themselves or the next guy completely. Tend to be literal, inflexible.

64

On Friday, for example, during the presession I suggested to Billy* that he gather some boys together and go out for a swift game of football. When he got outside the boys lost interest and wanted to go back in but Billy could not allow them to since I had suggested *football*. Unable either to carry out the original suggestion or to switch tacks, he got disgusted with himself, furious with the kids, and no doubt silently angry with me. The problem seems to be that "good" behavior is seen as that which is in accord with the boss's mandate. Billy, a bright kid, could have done very well if only he felt that thinking for himself was permissible.

The mothers were also at the pre- and postsessions but with me as chairman they took a distinctly secondary role. This was true during the program as well. As long as I'm around, people keep coming to me for direction. I am the Man.

On Wednesday, Mrs. Norma Hughes, who by now knows the program as well as anyone, said: "Oh, you mean that we *don't* have to check everything with you?"

"No, dammit," I assured her, "I have no authority over you, legal or otherwise."

As a stated policy this seems to make good sense but to carry it out is quite another matter. I keep feeling seduced into taking an active, dominant role. Just as often, however, I am the seducer. I get to feel like doing things myself just to make certain that they will get done "right."

Jim is probably correct about the need for an all-black outfit. On the other hand, why can't we all simply be people together? The liberal Quaker mode continues to attract me. (Clean fun and good fellowship.) Why do they always refer to me as "Doctor Belenky"? I have asked people to call me Bob . . . many times.

Funny. It reminds me of the *Wizard of Oz*. The scarecrow was so very intelligent but could not believe it. The poor, the Negroes — many that I've met — don't seem really to believe that they have magic and power and can make a difference. Insufficient reinforcement.

The anger, the sense of inadequacy, the fear, can perhaps be shaped and turned to enhance optimism, potency. Isn't that what psychotherapy is all about — to help people gain control of their lives, make and effectuate decisions, move toward self-realization? But what about unemployment, racism, being shoved down, out? Perhaps psychological effects are simply by-products. . . .

I've got about eight logs on the fire. It's getting cold tonight although it was a warm day. Perhaps the embers will last until morning. I hope it snows soon.

December 8, 1965

Belenky: Mrs. Searcy, what decision did the mothers make about their involvement in the afternoon program from now on?

Searcy: We decided to close up. On December twenty-first we're going to have a Christmas party. Then we will remain closed again until after Christmas.

Belenky: What! But, but, when is the last day?

Searcy: Yesterday. No one is going to be here today.

Belenky: No mothers are coming today? You won't let the children in today? How about the older kids?

Searcy: No one.

Belenky: What about Friday? We've already signed up for a movie.

Searcy: So we'll tell them to come back Friday.

Belenky: What about next week? There won't be any program? What are we going to do with the teen-agers?

Searcy: There will be a program on Friday and then no more until after Christmas. The mothers have

shopping to do, and some of them are getting
jobs in department stores.

Belenky: But *why* can't we let the little kids in *this*
afternoon anyway?

Reed: Listen, Belenky, if we're in business to get
people to make their own decisions, then this
should be one of the big moments of our lives!

*   *   *

December 8, 1965

Memorandum to: Senior Staff and Shadow Faculty
From: Henry Olds, Executive Director, Shadow Faculty
On Tuesday, December 7, the executive committee
of the Shadow Faculty met with the administrative officers
of the Harvard Graduate School of Education and the
Research and Development Center. . . . The group voiced
its approval for locating the Shadow Faculty facility in
Newton with the following provisions: that the bussing of
Negroes from Boston be included if possible. . . .

December 8, 1965; Group Meeting

Belenky: I want to report something to the group which
should be of interest. You ought to be kept informed about what we're doing over at the
University. Well, for one thing we're having
meetings. As you know, this program down
here is the first step toward what we once thought
was going to be an urban demonstration school —
elementary and high — to show school systems
what education can be. Well, we had a Shadow
Faculty meeting and we were talking about
where this school ought to locate. *Guess* where
they want to put it? *Newton*! The thing seems
so cockeyed to me that I don't know what to

say. But the fact is that you are getting screwed
again and you might as well know it and you
might as well try to do something about it.
And I don't know what to do.

December 9, 1965
A lot of us are upset over the decision. It was apparently
made by a small group of people without consulting anybody.
I wonder what it will mean for our program. . . .

* * *

Hi, Allen. Mathis.
How are you doing?
How do you like the job?
It's a nice job. I like it. I enjoy myself. I been
            helping little kids out with their painting, finger
            painting, being nice to the kids, hanging their
            coats up and so on. We're doing what we can
            for them. I think it's very nice that we're trying.
            So, what have you been doing, Josephine?
I've been helping Gail out and watching other teen-agers
            doing things with the children they have.
            On Monday or Tuesday afternoon I plan
            to start making Christmas wreaths for the kids.
How do you feel about the job generally?
It's interesting to see what the kids will do and if you don't
            give them something to do, to see what they do
            that way. I love kids and I love to work with
            them.
Tony, what are some of the things you've been doing?
I kind of entertain the kids in one way or another; help them
            out — anything like that. Sometimes I wonder
            what I'm doing. Like every day I get home from
            work and I say, What did I accomplish today?
            Yesterday I accomplished something. It was the

68

best day we had in a long time. I was entertaining the boys and girls with my guitar and then we
had a little dancing here and there. Something
different instead of coloring all day long. They
like it. Last night I really felt like something,
no kidding.

How about you, Arthur?

Most of the time I think about what we're going to do with the
kids.

Well, what do you do?

When they first come in I sit them down at a table. If they
want to do art I sit them at an art table. If they
want to read books I sit them at a storybook
table. If they want to make things I put them at a
table where they're making things. But mostly
I find out what they want to do. Then I send them
to an aide where it's happening at.

What about you, Gail, what're you doing?

I have "The Missionettes," a young teen girls' club, on Tuesdays
and Thursdays, and I have a group of little kids
during the other days. We draw and make different
things. The Missionettes are giving a dinner tonight
and they're going to put on a play.

*　*　*

December 8, 1965

Memorandum to: The Shadow Faculty

From: Bob Belenky

Re: The Big Rush

I would like to suggest that we hold our horses. ∧

The problem as I see it is that we still have no consensus
about the kind of school we should be operating and the
choice of site may prematurely determine the nature of the
institution.

My message, briefly, is "whoa!"

69

Homework questions:
1. Do we want a school which tries to teach autonomy, self-determination, and the uses of power both on a personal and social level, or are we interested in sponsoring vaguely Platonic dialogues which shy away from practical uses?
2. Are we interested in social and institutional change and if so what are the strategies which are worth considering?
3. Do we begin with pluralism or work toward it?
4. Do we work with the community and if so how?
5. Does the community work with us and even determine how we function?
6. Dare the school build a new social order?
7. How hot should our hothouse be?
8. Check one:
    A. Negroes and Boston Irish are ignorant and thus need to be educated.
    B. Negroes and Boston Irish are ignorant and therefore need social workers with food baskets.
    C. Negroes and Boston Irish have a distinctive body odor.

* * *

The Newton plan evaporated.

* * *

December 15, 1965
While rhetoric flew around Shadow Faculty meetings, Mrs. Searcy summed up conditions in the field this way:

70

Well, I think it has kind of slowed down right at this point. But after Christmas I feel like it's going to pick up. Everybody will be able to put more effort into it and more time. Of course, we've done a lot already. We fixed up a little reading room and a conference room. Hung pictures on the wall, got children's books and prints and a film.

I had a nice experience with a little girl who came down here with a baby-sitter and she didn't want to stay. She screamed and cried and I told the baby-sitter to go on. Within ten minutes she was quiet and reading a book and it made me feel good.

It seems like we are making some headway. When the little children come it seems like they like it very much.

I'd like to do creative things with the children. I have so many ideas. I'd like to give a Tom Thumb wedding, a fashion show. Things like that. And teach them, too.

We went to the Cambridge Friends School the other day and it was wonderful. So different from the schools I know. You walk in there and you feel at home. It's bright and I just loved it. The things they *do!* We went into one room and they had little fish. Crawfish, they called them, in a little pool. And they had marbleized plaques hanging on the walls. I understand that the children made these themselves. Then they had an afternoon program for all the children in the neighborhood. I think we can use some of their ideas for our own program!

After Christmas I think it will be wonderful here.

Christmas Party, 1965

It's very crowded
I'm looking for my little brother
Everyone wants a gift or something
It's a bloody mess. But a *happy* bloody mess.
To tell the truth, it don't actually look that well organized.
I didn't know we were going to have so many.
Everybody heard about the party and everybody showed up.
I don't know where my coat is.
Everybody in the other room! The cake is there!
Somebody stole my present!

* * *

December 25, 1965

Merry Christmas. . . .

I've never felt so depressed, low, miserable. . . . Jim Reed
and I had a horrendous argument. In fact, a series of them,
increasing in tempo and severity. Can we work together? I
swear that he pushed me on and on, further and further, with
his hostility and gratuitous anger until I got mad and then he
said that he saw the white man's snarl on my face just where
he knew it was all the time. I swear he *seeks out* defeat as
surely as the tree shrew seeks out its nest.

But that's *my side* of it.

His side is that I'm egotistical, insensitive, obtuse, white.

I wonder if there's some truth to his race shit.

I mean there are clearly qualities in him that I shall always
lack but envy. And for him there are probably similar things
about me.

But that's not the same as admitting to racism. Is this oaf
going to wreck everything? Will he trip over his own feet and
then say I tripped him?

How awful not to be seen as me but rather as a "white
man!" Like "nigger." Now maybe I can empathize.

72

But what can I say except, "You got me wrong. I am different."

* * *

Playroom 81 Ladies Discussing Their Visit to the Shady Hill School in Cambridge

February 3, 1966

"The buildings were, oh, they were something else, you know!"

"But the tuition! Nine hundred dollars in grade three!"

"And their science class! The kids had the microscopes outside and they were taking the snow and putting it on the slides and looking through it right there."

"They have all the different worms and bees and hornets and they get them right from around the school."

"From the pond."

"And they get their own clay. They dig it themselves!"

"The children do *every*thing themselves. It's wonderful!"

"Little kindergarten kids. They were sawing, hammering, using the drill. I just couldn't understand it."

"Everything was 'Do it your own way.' In the Boston Schools everything is, 'Do it the way the teachers *tell* you to do it!' "

"After they have their snack they get their mats out and lay on the floor and the teacher tells them a story. You get so engrossed in it that you just sit there. I forgot where I was and put my arm in a pot of clay. I was just as bad as the kids. The teacher was making it so real. And all the kids were sitting up like *this*. They were so interested."

"We could do a lot of things here that they do and it wouldn't take any money at all. Like get a bottle of Dazzle starch and let the children paint with it. When it's hardened, it makes a picture."

73

"One boy was planing down his wood and he was whistling. In our schools if you whistle, out you go!"

* * *

January 13, 1966

Gail Titus: All the mothers do is sit at home and watch dog-gone soap operas all afternoon long instead of getting up and getting themselves down here to do something so we can *get* some place. We've been here almost two months now — a little longer than that — and we've accomplished a little, but you know, I mean, we should have been much farther along by now. We should have this place painted and everything. Us teen-agers, we can't do all of it by ourselves. Well, if *they* don't start doing something, *I'm* going to get up and do something! We start moving; they'll start yelling. They always do when teen-agers try to do anything. Let them blow their brains out for all I care. Because this program is going to get started! This weekend I'm going to sit down and write out a schedule for next week and get the approval of the rest of the teen-agers when we come in on Monday. We're going to get this program going!

* * *

February 7, 1966; Up in New Hampshire

John:*   I'm going to tell you the truth. I'm full and warm and I've to tell the truth.

Tony: Confession Time.

John: I don't know what Lisa got but she really got some men. She's mighty attractive to a lot of boys. She's even got you sewed up, Arthur.

74

Arthur: Lisa just thinks she's cute, that's all. She's a little
spoiled but that's all right. Didn't you tell me that
you were spoiled, Lisa?

Lisa:* No.

Tony: She's got it made. Some spoiled people are all right,
you know.

* * *

Arthur's Song:
Rock me baby
Rock me baby
Rock me in your arm
When you rock me
Rock me with your charm
I just want to be
Like a little baby
When he going
To sleep

* * *

**Grievances Against Some of the Teen-Age
Aides (Boys, Mostly) by the Mothers**

April 4, 1966
Last straw
He was mad because the mothers wanted to hold a
meeting
Broke kids' toys
Dragged coke out of the cabinet
Also ate cookies
Used Mrs. Spriggs' cup
Left paint with scraps and so forth
Didn't clean up

75

Left it for the mothers
Threatened Gail with a knife
Undesirable talk in front of children
Jumped on toys to break them up
Kicked them one by one
Broke into Mrs. Spriggs' cabinet
Came out of the back room with his zipper down
Made a joke
Used foul talk
They were talking about having sexual relations
We as mothers can't say anything to them
They don't respect us
They just lost all respect for us
I don't think that we have to go on like this!

* * *

February, 1966, Jim Reed Talks to the Men

The big problem is the Negro organization of Negro men. All over the country the people who are least organized are Negro males. We need to get the Negro male. The Negro male hasn't been able to get employment. He hasn't been able to do do a lot of things and people have gotten to the point where they're just accustomed to not seeing him. Do you know that there's nothing that shakes a school up more than to have a husband show up one morning?

Voices: All the responsibilities have been pushed on the
woman
The women take care
They are the ones who have the money so they
run the race
But it's not the woman's fault
The women have been *put* ahead of the men
The women have been *put* in this kind of condition

The economic condition
Money
Where the man can't get a job and the woman can
When you've got money, that's what runs every-
thing

February, 1966; Jim Reed

Any time a Negro man and a white man work on a community program together, there is always some strain and feelings get torn and that's what is happening here. The attitude
among the mothers is that Bob is the power source and that
I have nothing. I more or less just sort of go along and do
what is suggested. This is the general thinking. When anything comes up that is of any importance in their lives they
look first at Belenky. *Dr.* Belenky. I think that the colored
mothers are not accustomed to seeing a Negro in a position
of authority — especially from an institution like Harvard.
They just can't seem to believe that this is the case. Especially since I'm not a university-trained person. The white
mothers are caught up in the same web but we won't know
what the white mothers *really* think until some friction arises.

The women go into the next room and they tell Bob their
problems. Jay, too. I mean something *important* that has to
do with their lives as people and as mothers, as a family.
These are the types of things they are very reluctant to come
to me with. I confronted one of the mothers with this and
she said, "Well, you know how it is." And I said, "No, I
don't know how it is." "Well, after all," she said, "that's the
Man, you know, and if anybody can do anything, *he* can do
it!"

The other thing that underlies all this is that I get the impression that I am a Negro and I know a little bit about
Negroes but Bob doesn't believe it. He really doesn't believe
that I know about Negroes. I've been one all my life. And
when I say something, it's after due deliberation. I don't say

77

I'm God but I do believe that I can come a little bit close to understanding them. Bob gives me no credit for that.

To say that none of this affects our working relationship down here is ridiculous. In a time of crisis it will make itself more manifest than it does now. I am certain that before it's over Bob will have occasion to learn firsthand that he represents the Great White Father and that he is expected to solve all ills. I have no authority, no magic, and I can do nothing. When it is all boiled down, I have to come to Bob to do it, to solve it. And to make matters worse, Bob *will* do it, solve it. When the time comes, he will solve it. And that's how the situation stands.

He supplies a need, there's no question about it. Whether it is because of his credentials, his ability, or his whiteness, I don't know. *He* feels it's my weakness and incompetence as a person, as a man. This is where we have trouble with each other. I *know* I am a man and I *know* I am capable of dealing with the situation. I also know I have had experiences, significant ones, and have learned things which Bob will never know because he was too busy getting his degrees. I have lived long enough to know what happens when a Negro can go to a white man and ask him for money or for help for himself or his community. Ultimately the Negro is weakened.

Don't you understand, Bob, that where you and I foul up is that I'm not accusing you of anything? I'm not saying that you were doing some evil magic tricks. I am merely describing the effect on me because of your background and my background and the backgrounds of the people we are trying to work with.

In this damned program I haven't been able to do anything — to get, to push a thing through, even when I try. So I'm accused of not being competent. I'm told to get rid of my inhibitions. Bob says, "Look, *I* did it. It was simple. You can do it, too."

I have never seen myself as a backward person nor have I ever missed trying to stand up and be counted when the opportunity presented itself.

But I know that Bob is still thinking: "Come on, old Jim. There's a lot you could have done but you just weren't man enough to try!"

* * *

February 9, 1966

Belenky: They were sitting around very pleasantly, listening to records, kind of cozy and happy. Then all of a sudden, out of the blue, Jim descended. He accused her of being irresponsible, incompetent. She got very angry. Our best teen-age aide!

Clark: Jim did all this without really consulting us. How upset *he* would have been if we had done something like that without consulting *him.* In the heat of battle Jim just *acted.*

Belenky: *Why* didn't I pull him aside and talk it over with him, tell him to calm down?

February 9, 1966

Reed: I can't get mad according to order. I'd had all I could take from that girl. You know what I mean? I've had *enough* of that girl! I don't need any kind of special training to know that.

It would not have gotten to that point if Bob had *entered* the conversation rather than sit there as if he were observing something under a microscope. He could *see* what was happening. It had gone as far as it could. That girl and I have been having arguments right along and those fellows act like they don't know anything about it.

February 13, 1966

Clark: Jim got up and said, "I've made my decision. I'm quitting. I'll send you my letter of resignation shortly!"

February 13, 1966

Belenky: He shoved the tape recorder aside and announced that he was withdrawing his resignation. Instead he would force me to fire him. "I'll make you *fire* me!" He told the mothers that my only purpose was to study them. He told them that even though he is nominally the program director, I had given him no power whatsoever and was using him simply as a wedge to gain entry into the Negro community. He said that I believed in exerting no control over the teen-agers.

This all took me by surprise and, frankly, it scared me. His manner was stormy and his words were hard to swallow. It hurt. He sees me as a bigot.

February 13, 1966

Reed: I'm not writing a book on this. This is inside of me and I've had all I can handle. You see what I mean? Some things I can sit up and discuss like it is a *thing*. But this has to do with a lot of things. They've already put limitations on what we can talk about and I've put mine on, too, and they don't jell. It's Belenky's project and he says he's not going to get rid of any teen-agers.

I feel that no matter what happens in this program I am kind of like in left field by myself. Those two guys have some sort of an idea or thing that I just can't seem to break through on. We're not really together.

February 13, 1966

Belenky: There was enormous tension between Jim and myself the rest of that day.

I'm going to have to try hard to stay out of the
way and let Jim swing with the program. But I
don't really trust him.

April 4, 1966

Reed: I don't think those fellas *ever* trusted me. There is
always this feeling that I am being approached by
two people. I don't give a damn. But it sure is an
aggressive atmosphere. I don't like the image those
fellows are trying to paint of me.

I solve some of my problems by getting out and
just walking and kicking them around and talking
to myself and walking the dog. And finally I come
back and I have some idea of where I want to go.

It's like that idiot at the Shadow Faculty meeting turning to me and saying, "You dig that, man?"
I don't "dig" any goddamned thing. I'm just a man
like he is and I resent that condescending bullshit.
I don't use that kind of vocabulary with him.

There are a whole lot of things like that just eating away at me. Maybe I don't want to be classified
statistically.

April 4, 1966

Clark: I don't see that our disagreeing has to hurt each
other. I mean granted we are hurting each other
right now. But disagreeing and being angry don't
necessarily have to go together. If we can ever get
to the point where we trust each other enough to
disagree without being mad, we will have something that is really great. It is something that very
few people have because they are so pissed at each

81

other and so mistrustful. The fact that some people are Negro and some are white only accentuates it.

We really will be cooking with gas if we ever get to that point. We will have valves for getting things out so that things don't come to the point where there is just this anger that destroys. I feel that I haven't been as frank with Jim as I wish I had been this year. I feel that there have been times when I have mistrusted him or haven't said what was on my mind because I wasn't sure how he would take it. I didn't trust him enough to let him have it at times. I'm not too happy about that.

I don't want to hurt him or play games with him. I am uncomfortable playing games. I think he is, too. One of the reasons we get fouled up is that none of us are any damn good at playing games. Thank goodness we're not. That's one of our strengths. We are really pretty honest guys.

My ambition is to be able to sound off and to trust the other guy enough to know that sounding off won't blow things up.

* * *

March 28, 1966
One bright spot: The mothers remain enthusiastic and really consider the Playroom *their* program, which indeed it is. And they keep coming forward with great ideas. It is almost as if the battles among the Harvard guys don't really bother anybody because it isn't *our* program anyway. We're just a bunch of crazy men from Mars.

February 14, 1966; Mrs. Faith Harding
Since we formed the teen-agers to work with their own groups

of children and the mothers have their own groups, things have been much better. Everybody is doing something now. The teen-agers know they belong. They make up their minds what they're going to do with their children. They work with them well and it's been coming out all right. Before this they felt left out. They were not too happy to work with us because, well, sometimes we had to tell them what to do. I guess that's what's wrong with a lot of kids nowadays. They think we're telling them too much. So we give them a little responsibility. That's the only way.

We have sixty-four children that are signed up now for the afternoon program. But there is another problem. One day we don't have so many and on another day we'll have maybe the whole sixty-four. But we know why that is. A lot of children go to tutoring at St. John's and they're not back until late. I think we're going to have to plan around that.

We get some frisky little boys, Wow! They'll work on this just *so* long and oh, boy, they'll want to go over there and do something else. We have to learn how to handle that.

Well, I'll tell you about little children. You put them all together and they wouldn't care if you're green, orange, or yellow until someone like us comes along and says, "Don't you play with Suzy!" That's the way it is. Like if I read in the paper about some little kid getting hurt, I don't know what color he is or who he is. I sit down and cry because I have children and I'm a mother and I feel for that person.

I got on this program because I wanted to help my own children and, because I learned a lot of things that would help them, I found that I could be helping other children down here also.

There's still a lot of equipment that we need but the program is pretty good.

* * *

**Four Years Later: Reminiscences of Playroom 81
January, 1970; Mrs. Joyce Pulley and Mrs. Dody Lewis**

Mrs. Pulley: We started out with ten mothers and now
we're down to three. The morning preschool
program is really in full swing. The children
love it. Today one lady said that her children
talk about us when they go home. They say
we're full of love and understanding. It's a
good feeling.

Mrs. Lewis: The afternoon program has kind of gone
downhill with only the two of us running it. We
don't have anyone to do all the things that we
would like to do. Maybe that's why we have less
children — only about four or five are here now —
because we really don't have enough help to keep
them active.

Mrs. Pulley: If we had the staff I'd like to see a full program again. The place used to be jammed. We used
to serve hot chocolate and popcorn. And we used
to play games. The place was really going! Now
it's fine in the mornings but dead in the afternoons.
Barbara Searcy has a better job for a year. We
can't hire any more mothers because the
Commonwealth Service Corps has cut down on
funds and they're cutting back on their help and
they're dropping some of the organizations they've
been working with. I think that the Playroom will
be one of them. That's why we can't find anyone
else. The three of us — Dody, myself, and a lady
who works only mornings — are carrying the load.
It's so discouraging. Nobody wants to work for
nothing. Here I am. I like what I'm doing. Been
going every day for four years. At Christmas time
my money was so low I really was very depressed.

I've been offered other jobs — Head Start aide,
nursery school teacher — but this is something *we*
started. It's part of the community and I just don't
want to drop it. Loyalty, I guess. I don't know
how long our loyalty will last.

Mrs. Lewis: Maybe if we could get government funding we
could run the preschool a little bit longer and then
mothers could leave their kids here and a lot more of
them would be able to get jobs. But there's no
money around for this kind of project. We can't be
licensed in the basement and we didn't want to
move away from the neighborhood. None of us
have degrees and that makes it difficult, too.

Mrs. Pulley: But it's been a very good thing for me. It's
gotten me out of the house. I've met all sorts of
people through the Playroom. It's given me
opportunities that I never would have had if I
stayed at home. It's been a challenge.

Mrs. Lewis: In a way it's much easier to keep busy than to
sit around and do nothing. Here I've learned things
about myself and my own kids. Handling another
person's kid you have to treat them a little bit differ-
ently than you treat your own. With your own you
can speak with a firmer hand because they're your
own. With someone else's child you've got to play
around a little, kind of praise the things they do —
you know, make them feel they're loved and
they're smart. It's strange seeing them do what you
want with just a little softer way of speaking to
them. With your own kids you can really be yourself but with someone else's you have to treat them
accordingly.

Mrs. Pulley: When they see us in the street, they call to us.
You know, it's a nice feeling because it isn't your
relatives or your own children calling to you. It's

85

a strange kid that a few weeks ago you didn't even know and they're waving to you and pointing you out to their mother or their friends. It's really nice. Funny. Before I got involved in the Playroom, I always wanted my children to go outside and play so I could have free time to myself. Now I love being with children — even my own! I didn't know that I could take command. We have gone on bus trips and everything and to have the reponsibility for so many children is frightening but you find that you really can do it once you put your mind to it. It has been very rewarding to find myself in a new role.

Mrs. Lewis: We are playing three roles: mother, teacher, and baby-sitter.

Mrs. Pulley: When they climb up on you, they want you to comfort them and hug them and love them. I'm really surprised at myself. Really. I hated to be bothered with preschoolers. Now even when I was on vacation I came down to the Playroom. I'd come on down to the Playroom when I should have been home on vacation! I just like it. I really do.

Mrs. Lewis: The Playroom helped me to get involved. I was sitting at home twenty-four hours a day doing nothing, eating and getting fatter and fatter. From the refrigerator to the television. Then when I had my littlest one — Carla — I wanted someplace for her to be with kids her own age so I started getting involved.

Mrs. Pulley: During my years with the Playroom I've had my ups and downs. The Playroom meant so much to me that when things didn't go right it upset me so bad that I was really hurt because it was part of something I had started. At one point some in-truders from the suburbs came in and we were just put aside in a little corner. I felt terrible because we weren't consulted about anything. Plans were made for us without asking us how, why, and how we felt about anything. I almost left the Playroom. I thought that I had put in too much of my time to be left out all of a sudden. Everything I did was for the Playroom. I begged things and borrowed — all for the Playroom. I'm always saying: "Can I have this for the Playroom?" or "I need some paper towels for the Playroom" or "I need some soap for the Playroom." And they always said: "Oh, here comes Joyce. I wonder what she wants this time?" But as long as I was doing it for the Playroom I didn't care what they said.

Mrs. Lewis: It was going for about two months when I joined. Remember back how the place was a dark green and a light green? Remember how we used to make that plaster and how Jim Reed taught us how to make molds? Remember the classes we used to have and the coffee and the lunches. Oh, and the painting and the painting and the painting. It looked like we'd never get finished painting it. It was so much a familylike thing. It was really fun.

Mrs. Pulley: The thing that stands out most in my memory was when cute Ted Kennedy came down to visit us. Ooooooooooo — he was a *doll*! Remember the bus trip out to Grotonwood with the kids when we had the snowball fights?

Mrs. Lewis: Remember those discussions with Jay Clark? We used to have the gripe sessions. They were good. We didn't think they were so good at the time. And the times we all went out to lunch together. Remember when we went out to Camp Stowe, walking through the woods, inspecting the property? Remember the fund-raising parties?

Mrs. Pulley: There were bad times, too. Remember when

Bob passed out a paper he wrote about us to the Shadow Faculty without first letting us see it? We called a meeting and felt that he had betrayed us. We had some bitter feelings for a while but we eventually ironed things out and became friends again.

Mrs. Lewis: The two mothers who were white — Ann Paige and Pauline Kuhn — were just like us. I mean they held our kids, we held their kids. We ate at their houses, they ate at our houses. When I was under strain one day and was having company, they came over and helped me get the house straight.

Mrs. Pulley: They talk to our kids just like they talk to their own kids. When my Tony sees Pauline, it's just like he's seeing one of his aunts. It's just like they're one of the family.

Mrs. Lewis: I'd hate to let the Playroom go down.

Mrs. Pulley: All the work we put into it. I'd hate to give it up like that. Barbara Searcy says she'll be back after a year but I don't think so. Everyone wants to move ahead. I guess this is the chance for her to. I don't blame her. I would, too. But once *I* make my mind up to leave, I don't think I'd say that I'd be back within a year. If I went and got used to getting a salary, I don't think that I'd commit myself to coming back.

Mrs. Lewis: That's true, because you'd probably depend on your salary once you started getting it. Just like I got to depend on the $36.92 that I get every two weeks from the Playroom.

The Searcys

Barbara Searcy: We had a lot of theories. First we just wanted to baby-sit so that mothers could go to the laundromat or go to the store. That didn't work

88

out. Some of the mothers wouldn't come back to pick up their kids.

All kinds of theories. We changed things weekly almost. Then we hit upon the idea of having pre-schoolers in the morning and an afterschool program for older kids. It has worked out just beautifully.

There is real learning going on here. It is not just a place to leave kids. The children use Play Doh, puzzles, and, you know, whatever you see in most good nursery schools. We didn't depend on one theory — like Montessori. We tried to improvise according to the children's needs. We had dancing, for example; they did exercises. Punchy, what else did you do in the afternoon program?

Punchy Searcy (aged seven): Boxing, ooooooooo — *ex*ercises and stuff. We played games. I cooked spaghetti, made cookies.

Angela Searcy (aged ten): Cookies. We had some chicken, some greens, and some mashed potatoes, some cinnamon rolls and baked macaroni — I mean macaroni salad. Let's see, what else? We had breakfast — French toast for breakfast.

Punchy: Yup.

Angela: And we had taffy apples and deviled eggs.

Mrs. Searcy: There were four of us. I think the uniqueness of the Playroom was the fact that it was parents. You know, the kids could see us down in the Play-room and then at six or seven o'clock they could see us in the store buying a loaf of bread. It wasn't somebody from the outside coming in. It was us, people they knew. I think this was the really good thing about it.

Angela: The best thing I liked about it was teaching the pre-schoolers. I made papers for them. I read books to them. I'd put a picture of a cloud on the chalk-board and a picture of rain and a picture of snow and a picture of the sun. Then I'd ask them, "What kind of day is it outside?" And they would tell me. Then I'd ask them, "What would you wear on this kind of day?" And they would tell me.

Mrs. Searcy: I had a ten-year-old boy I used to teach once. In turn he was teaching me Hebrew. He had the book. I could see what a small child feels like look-ing at the alphabet for the first time. Here I was looking at something I never saw before. I didn't understand it but I think I got to page four before I left. It was beautiful. He was my teacher. He was teaching me and I let him know that I don't know everything. It was really a nice experience. He came every lunch hour just as faithful as could be. It got so I became really interested in it. Adults have really got to bring themselves down to where the kids are. I just had fun. I had more fun there than anything else.

I think it would be good to get some of the mothers who would like to go out to work to use the Playroom as a training center in child care where their children could also be involved just as ours were involved. The mother would be out of the house. She would be earning some money and learning a job skill. She would be with her own child and the child would be in a learning situation. You could just keep going on and on with this if you just sat down and thought about it.

I've seen so many new things recently that I didn't even realize were on the market. I would love to make use of them down here. There are new new games out — like Soma, mathematical games where a child is playing but also learning. A child

90

is in school all day. When he comes home he doesn't want to go to a tutoring program. But there are ways that a child can learn and not even realize it. He would be playing but his mind would be working and he would be learning. Play is so constructive! With proper use of these materials, a child's experience here at the Playroom could be fantastic.

I have so many ideas that I'd like to try out here.

Thoughts about Education
January, 1970;
Jim Reed

I still very strongly doubt that it is possible for me as a black man to get involved with a white man in a black project in which he's boss. I must have my own thing to do or I'm not going to work with him.

There were problems with the Playroom. I still think there should have been more demonstrations on the part of the mothers to confront the power structure and to get the hell out of the basement. The mothers had a lot on their side and an administrator would have a very difficult time saying "no" to them. Bob and I had different philosophies. A black man in charge would have gotten the mothers up in arms down to City Hall!

The younger generation is challenging institutions, the police, and the whole damned society. Yet it's funny that when you talk to these kids they readily admit that you've got to have some law and order. Recently I was involved in a study with Arthur D. Little in which we tried to determine optimal ways of training police officers in Cambridge. I thought we ought to interview kids. I'd find ten or fifteen playing in the alleys and would get them into a conversation about the police. They wanted a number of things from the police.

Mostly respect. When I suggested that perhaps we ought to do away with cops they said, "Oh, no, of course not." I said, "You say they're no good. So why have them at all? Why not just get rid of them?" They said, "We need them. They keep order. They direct traffic and help little kids and old ladies across the street!"

And they meant it. It's very interesting. The same kids that people lambast on television and in the newspapers for being opposed to law and order are simply thinking, evaluating human beings and they are asking questions that cannot be answered on the end of a nightstick.

Everybody wants law and order. But adults don't care whether it comes on the end of a stick or the end of a hose. The kids do care.

If I had my way I'd like to take very rough black kids and white kids out to the country and develop them physically and mentally into polished little gentlemen and then send them back into the community. I would take kids who could see that there is some sense in learning math and who could understand that to be without it is a serious handicap. I'd take them and teach them. And I'd see to it that they came out of it with good manners, whether they wanted to have them or not; whether they choose to use them or not. But, damn it, to be *able* to be neat and clean and to dress well and act well *is* tremendously important. I'd like to see the kids become Renaissance men — people who have an appreciation for a number of things: art, music, science, history, engineering, literature — and then I'd turn them loose and let them do what they wanted to. I would not allow them to be put in a box.

I cannot buy the argument that bringing someone to the country is wrong because they're doomed to live their lives in the city. If a doctor finds a person suffering from tuberculosis in dirty, stinking squalor, they don't try to perform a cure where he is. They take him out and put him in a hospital where he can get a grip on things, and only then do they send him back. Sometimes you've got to get a person away from the thing that defeats him.

I think that a sort of mini Outward-Bound program ought to be tied up with every school program — particularly those in poor communities. I think of a school program as building in elements speaking to the problem of self-image. A school should help a kid begin to feel that he is somebody and that he's got something to offer and yet be able to fit back into the system if that's what he wants to do.

If Bob really wanted to do something he would start a school. All of the Jewish heritage he is a part of is very important. A Jew cannot tolerate ignorance. He has a respect for learning and would bring pressure to bear on the children. School on Saturday, school on Monday, school on Tuesday, school on Wednesday and Thursday and Friday; the building up of respect and a feeling for the importance of learning. Who knows what could happen once that ball gets rolling?

May 19, 1970;
Jay Clark Reminisces
The thing that excited us during the spring of 1965 was the thought that instead of sitting around and dreaming with the Shadow Faculty about what education *could* be, we were going to have an opportunity to set up a real school, a storefront in a real community, a laboratory in which we could test our ideas, a place to get our hands dirty, a school which would reach out to everyone instead of being dry and insular — no nineteenth-century brick fortress with locked doors!

We began with our expectations and biases. Certainly we wanted to involve the community — but in implementing *our* ideas.

At first Jim was rather quiet, sizing us up, getting a feel

for the realism of our plans. Jim was concerned from the very beginning that we work *with* the community and that the program be a disciplined one, that it be structured. He was afraid of another sloppy, meaningless project in the black community.

Bob and I thought that we would like to start a storefront learning center run by teen-agers who would somehow teach younger children. We thought that there might also be informal classes going on where people from the community might drop in when they wanted to. It was to be a sort of avant-garde coffeehouse with education for entertainment which would help kids get to where they wanted to go. The fantasy part of it was the imagined ease with which this was to be accomplished. We didn't know the community and we vastly overestimated our own abilities.

Well, we advertised ourselves as a program for young children, so mothers in the area began to drop in. A lot of them. Curious. Interested in checking us out. Interested in checking out the teen-agers. We drank coffee with the mothers and we talked about kids and how to handle them. Pretty soon we were running informal seminars on topics like "How to Read to Kids," "How to Control Rambunctious Preschoolers," and so forth.

We began to feel that the mothers who came down were worth keeping on as part of the program.

We then had on our staff two groups — mothers and teen-agers — who were often in conflict. The mothers saw the teen-agers as delinquent and hostile (some of them were), and the teen-agers saw the mothers as unreasonable and nagging (some of them were). In disgust, the teen-agers would retreat to the back rooms and play records and the mothers would commandeer the front room, drink coffee, and gab.

As I look back on all the work that was done, I would say that the development of the mothers' part of the program was the most important thing. The fact that they have continued on their own, that the Playroom still exists today, penniless, five years after it began, that it is still going strong with far more organization and purpose than ever, testifies to our ability — Bob's, Jim's, and mine — to bungle things up enough for the mothers to realize that they would *have* to take over!

It was important, too, that we began to share some of our own skills with the mothers. My background is in clinical and school psychology. I spent much time with the mothers, going over some of the tests used in clinics or in school where their kids were having problems. We went over these tests, mothers had a chance to administer them, to make up their own, to observe a child in our preschool class for ten or fifteen sessions and then to write a report on that child. The mothers got to know how a psychologist thinks and how critically to evaluate his role. They also learned something about teachers. Perhaps most exciting of all, they came to discover some of the skills they themselves had as mothers. Many of them were able to perform far more effectively with difficult children than many of the best clinicians I've seen in this town. They knew how to listen to a child and to understand what he is experiencing and feeling.

Bob, Jim, and I learned something about the organization necessary to set in motion a program — even a small one. I think we learned a lot about patience and humility.

I came away convinced that the best role for me is "resource person" rather than "consultant" or "director." A consultant is always trying to nudge people into doing what he wants done. A director is better only because he's more open about his purposes. A resource person, on the other hand, is someone who is available to another person when needed. Otherwise, both go peaceably about their business.

We, unfortunately, were sometimes incompetent directors, at other times uncertain consultants. But eventually we became resource people. Our biggest handicap was that we were terribly anxious for our program to succeed.

I think that Bob and I had a fantasy of marching in,

getting a grand thing going, and then magnanimously turning it over to the natives. We were like British colonial governors. We did everything but wear shorts and white stockings.

If I had to do it over, I would start by going first to the community and involving it from the beginning in the development of plans for the program. I would work slowly. I would try to be painfully honest about what we were giving to the community and what we expected from it in return. I would be inclined to draw up a specific contract specifying benefits to both parties. For the mothers it might have been a guarantee of paid employment following work at the Playroom or an opportunity to obtain real credentials that might be negotiable elsewhere.

Bob and I can get jobs pretty much wherever we want without great difficulty. But I've noticed that it's not that easy when you're born poor.

Chapter Three

SUMMER INTERLUDE

Searching for Utopia

I worked in camps a lot. For about twelve years. During high
school and college and the summer Alice was born and then in
the summer of 1968 at the Morgan Memorial Fresh Air Camp,
a large place for poor kids exclusively. At Morgie I ran a
teacher-training "institute" with Boston College sponsorship. Any counselor could register at Boston College for one
or two courses that they could take in the camp setting. One
we advertised as "Special Problems of the Urban Child" and
the other, "Practicum in Camp Counseling." I was a professor
in residence and taught at night around campfires.

* * *

June 2, 1968

The camp, the camp, the camp.

The camp is my paradise. We will have a boat and talk
business afloat. Then in the evenings we will gather in Lindsay
Cottage and talk until morning about the kids and the times
and how and what to do.

I would like to soar. I would like to speak above a whisper,
in clear tones, to say what needs to be said, to inspire, to transcend rhetoric and cliches, to lift humanity, to lift myself and
stand on new ground. And to make sense and to get down to

what really is important. But not simply to talk. To act, to create, to develop. And why *not* a New Jerusalem?

* * *

Notes from Various Counselors' Journals

Expectations:

May 11, 1968
Went to Morgie today for a picnic and a tour of the camp. The people seem nice — as nice as people can seem on the first meeting. I look at them and wonder why they are here — why they are motivated to give a summer to city kids.

B. is out of her mind with the dirt of it all and is convinced that there are rats in the buildings.

Dr. Belenky has boxes of books and we can take the one we want home and I find that exciting. What happiness to dig through boxes of books and just borrow what you want.

I feel a vague excitement to be a part of something so big.

May 27
Inside, the thought of having to deal with children scares me. I must admit that it is the "in" thing to do. I live a false existence because I try to convince myself that it is great and so involving to be in urban education. I appear so involved and committed. What a farce!

Orientation:

June 21
I think the biggest problem I'm going to have is being a counselor instead of one of the kids!

The realization struck me that today is *the* first time I have ever talked to a colored person. I felt quite natural to be talking to one.

Tonight's discussion, I'm sorry to say, was very uninteresting to me. The group tried to toss the main topic around but it was dry.

June 22

Though I worked with inner-city kids last summer, I still don't know "them." In many ways I guess they're a lot like all kids but yet we *know* that they're different. Do you have to act different with them? You can't *fake* anything — have to act *naturally.*

I have been cleaning the bunk today. It's a real hard, dirty, icky job but I loved it.

I'm already tired of the gushy atmosphere they are trying to create here. Love, warmth, compassion and understanding, yes! But not like a drooling old dog!

June 23

The science fellow from the Educational Development Corporation was very interesting. It was while we were playing with his materials that I felt for the first time that I wasn't afraid. I got so wrapped up in the things we were doing I forgot to be afraid. That makes me think of how stimulating our programs must be for the children so they will get so wrapped up in what they are doing that they'll forget to be afraid.

How does a counselor react when she knows that just to hug a child would not be the best thing to do at the moment? What are some other ways to let the child know you are concerned and want him for your friend?

The idea that scares me the most is that kids can see through to the real me. I'm scared I'm not being myself and I want to find myself.

What can I offer? I can listen. I will listen to these kids and take what they say seriously.

June 24
I really feel dumb. Some of us were sitting around talking about welfare, Black Power, and socialism in Sweden. I could contribute nothing but listened greedily to others' ideas. Never have I had such enlightening experiences. I am so excited and want to learn so much.

It's the SAME damn stuff of lecture, group discussion, etc. I'm so fed up with trying to get to know people through talking in large groups. I feel everybody puts on a mask in such a group and I'm *scared* of large groups! I do hereby resolve to meet people individually or in small groups.

Education should basically involve the continual examination of assumptions and the adoption of more appropriate ones. The acquisition of information by itself has little to do with helping people do what they need to do because each of us fits the information he receives into assumptions we desperately cling to for protection against the void of existence and the anxiety that its awareness produces. A close friend's death challenges our assumptions. We become depressed. Normally, however, our protection consists in not knowing, in apathy, in rigidity. We do not love fully. We do not trust fully. We ignore.

It was interesting to observe that in at least three of the small discussion groups a black person was explaining things to white listeners.

June 25
Tonight my friends and I smiled, delighting in the delicate

summer rain. Night sounds are softened as if everything were packed in cotton. Raindrops softly patter on my slicker and slide onto my wet tennis shoes and everything is wet with the wonder of it. Frogs make love in the lush, dripping grass and send their cries through the night.

Last night was informative for basically the same reasons that it was embarrassing. I reacted as vehemently as some others. I usually do when I talk about race. Nevertheless I was at least mildly surprised that it became such a big thing. Perhaps my surprise was due to a conceited faith in my ability to size things up at a glance. Looking at camp I thought, "Oh, boy, this is great! I can forget about being black!" I thought I could throw off all those guards and stop being cynical. I fooled myself. I was thrown back immediately into assuming the guards again, speaking objectively and checking my words.

I keep thinking about that big discussion last night. It was great to see everyone so involved and to be emotionally involved myself. But the more I look back on it, the more struck I am with the feeling that all of a sudden there were real barriers between black and white. Like the blacks were saying, "Don't talk to me about prejudice . . . you don't know anything." The blacks give me the feeling that this "oneness" we're trying for is impossible. This really bothers me. I'm terribly idealistic and think that people can accept each other by common interests, personality, etc., no matter what color they are. One of the black counselors and I were talking about this afterwards. She says her experiences have shown that intelligent, unprejudiced people come out of a working relationship with blacks more bigoted. Why do I want her as a friend? Do I admire her or do I want to know a Negro? Are you prejudiced if you pity kids who live in Roxbury? Are you prejudiced only if you burn crosses? Are you bigoted if you seek out Negro friendships? I'm getting very confused.

101

Tonight (very, very late) my husband and I were talking with two fellow staff members. The setting was the kitchen. The conversation became quite intimate, each of us sharing past hurts and family problems. This I feel was the natural result of the previous night's heated group discussion. It was neat.

I've been a counselor for many years and increasingly the simplistic answers I used to give become more and more meaningless so that now I'm not totally convinced that we do more good than harm, dragging kids away from homes most of them don't really want to leave, dragging them away from parents with whom they at least know how to act and setting them down in the midst of 180 do-gooding acres with four butterflies to hover around them — telling them that they, too, may metamorphize if they just try hard enough. And even the ones who do very much want to come here are treated to something of the value of which I am not certain.

What the hell am I doing here?

How possibly to love, live, and work with one person — e.g. husband — 24 hours each day? I hate groups. He thrives on them. The anxiety and tension from lack of solitude builds — doesn't come in waves but builds. Fatigue is a problem here and probably increases the feeling of infringement by groups, schedules, pressure to perform.

June 26: Yet More Orientation
Depression. Want to take flight to Boston.

I stepped on an ant but didn't kill it right away and didn't care to end its suffering. Who said last night that children are basically nice and that counselors can "explain" to them that it's easier to be nice than to be cruel. What a naïve bitch she is! It's so much *harder* to be nice than cruel.

Reality isn't square or flat or triangular. It's round, it's cornerless and endless, and it's easy to go round on it but you're too dizzy to get off, and why have periods and sentences and capital letters because they're all lying? They are proclaiming an order that isn't there. It's a farce, man. Those neat little sentences tell you nothing but lies.

Man goes into traps more easily than fish. I just realized this making my first fish trap. Barn party! We danced and sang and drank until around eleven. Then some of us went to one of the cabins where we held a seance. Very cool. We called back one Miss Annie Brown and by god she came! Then K did some stage hypnosis as he drank beer. I drank scotch and water. Felt good! Got to be two in the morning so I left after hearing a discussion on what to do if a child swears or calls someone a name or is involved in a fight. I judged this discussion inconclusive . . . so I left.

We really worked hard around here today and it's shaping up. Boy, is it *dirty*!!

At first I felt sort of boxed in, claustrophobic in the wide open spaces, if that's possible. But now that I sense so much life around me, I feel better.

Enter the Children:

July 20
Morning. "Millie peed in the bed and she *lied*. She said she didn't and we felt her pants and theys are *wet*. She is a fuckin' liar. Millie, move you fuckin' pissed body outta here!" Millie cries because no one wants to play with her. I think she is faking, but as she lifts her face from the pillow I can see that she is really hurt. "Theys are gonna drown me at swimmin!" she says between wails. It is funny to me and I want to laugh. What is real and important to children is often funny to adults. I must remember though that Millie and each of the children is a person with needs and hopes and fears who wants to be loved.

103

Thought for today — let the children do things for you. It's great to give to them but it's just as important to take from them.

The kids seem to feel privileged to be in the choir. Once we got under way the music and their making it kept them going.

Tonight two of the other girls and I went to Omer's for a couple of drinks. We definitely need more single male counselors on campus, we decided. In a situation like this a woman needs a man whom she can confide in and trust. There are so many feelings that are left unshared because of the lack of desirable males. The married couples make us jealous because they have each other.

I do not like all adults I meet and it is imperative that I remember that I will not like all children.

I think this is a place worth throwing my whole self into for the sake of the campers. This is a place that can really make a difference in a child's life — and in a counselor's. It is really neat to see a camper gain more self-confidence as he works with his fellow campers. It is also neat to enjoy a camper individually and as a member of a group.

August 12, 1968
There is trouble here and I don't know if it's worth the bother of getting upset. But I am. This whole black-white thing is getting under my skin. It's a little late in the day to think of removing one's self from the problems of the world. The world is too small for one not to be touched by what goes on in the opposite corner. We can't conclude that we won't have the same problems here that we have in the cities. Why can't we be honest with ourselves? Why adopt a party line? Why say color makes no difference if it *does*? I can't stand this dishonesty.

104

It seems that the black counselors have some common problems and have been abused by the rest of us. This was news to me but when I tried to find out the specific gripes I got the feeling that people were saying, "If you can't see it yourself, we can't explain it to you." This disturbed both my wife and me.

I've grown up in a white town and went to white schools. I'm white-oriented. I'm just beginning to understand the black community. Hell, I'm just beginning to understand myself.

This summer I have gained a better understanding of the Black Power movement. It sounds to me that this could be most effective if it doesn't become distorted to the point where whitey becomes the underdog. But then, I have my white middle-class tradition supporting me, so why shouldn't the soul brother be allowed his?

I think that E. is very insecure (except at bullying, fighting) and needs real encouragement — gentle and sensitive encouragement in all areas except fighting. I think that giving him responsibility like I have in arts and crafts (and he also helps with horses, I understand) helps him a lot, too, although you have to be careful. You have to watch him when you give him responsibility.

I quit last week but as I think back I think I could have been good at this child thing but Morgie was just too much too soon. I wish in a way that I was still in the program so that I could find out. I still think I can be a good teacher and with time and work an excellent one.

What kind of stupid idiotic fool am I to think that I could competently teach black children or any children for that matter? I'm a dumb, stupid cookie with a lot of pious intentions but I'm not going to do a damn bit of good in the black society and I might as well concentrate on teaching poor white kids — but I'll probably mess up their lives, too.

I was thinking tonight that I can very honestly say that I even can appreciate the frustrations involved with this job because like I said with tears, it means something. Your frustrations and tears are justified. It's not the kind of feeling that comes from the usual, ordinary crappy sort of job. The upsets and those really dumpy feelings are *worth* experiencing and crying about because they are important; because what is more important to me than my kids?

On the way home we filled our jars with different kinds of moss, tiny trees, mushrooms, checkerberry plants . . . the result was great little terrariums. It was not just the fact that they had discovered that there's a continuous cycle of gasses which allows plants to survive but it was rather as Joan* said, "You know, we're taking part of Morgie back to the city. I can run over to my friends and show them what Morgie looks like. This is *so exciting*! They've never seen Morgie before." Indeed, Joan was right. I think, too, that this project meant more to them than any other.

* * *

The Children Speak

When the days are very long
I sit around singing a song
I sometimes try to cry
As if I'm going to die.
Almost every day
I begin to say
"I am really lonely
Am I the only . . .

106

One that is sad?"
Though I sometimes get mad.

> A turtle is funny
> it walks funny
> and it looks funny.
> I like turtles.
> I like to cech
> them.

I think camp is a lot of fun. You go on hikes, campouts,
swimming every day. That's why I think camp is fun. I like
best of all boating, fishing, arts and crafts, and camping out-
doors. On Saturday we went to a park. We rolled down a hill
and got stuck with thorns. We had a lot of fun. On Monday
night we had a party with the boys. We had a lot of fun. We
put salt and pepper in each other's hair. One boy took another
boy's spaghetti and threw it in his face. Then we had a party
with them. We went dancing hors d'oeuvres. That morning my
mother wrote and told me I have a new baby sister. I am very
happy.

> Columbia Point is dirty. It's got too many bad boys
> around Columbia Point. Every night the kids in our hall-
> way pull out the lights and beat kids up. I stay in and
> watch T.V. Sometimes my brother goes out and leaves me
> and my sister in the house by ourselves. And we feel
> scared. The Paul A. Dever is a nice school to go to. You
> can get lunch without paying and you can ask your
> teacher, "Can I get a drink?"

It was on a Monday I found a bird. I fed the bird every day. I
clean the box every day. She is a baby bird. She cries a lot. She
fell from the nest. She eats a little food. The baby bird went
to the bathroom in my hand.

> I felt sad and angry and I was nervous inside.
> The stars come out at nighttime and follow you.
> In Boston you can hear all them people yelling.

107

> You can hear the girls and boys playing and yelling and
> screaming and crying
> At their mother
> Because someone has taken their bike.
> When the moonlight comes out, the stars come out and
> shoot in the sky.

On my walk down the road I felt that we have a beautiful
world. When the cars go by I feel a breeze. I felt very sad when
I saw the chipmunk in the road dead. He probably got run over.
And to see his insides it was scary. I saw pretty things like the
trees swaying. I saw a snapping turtle, rabbits and I saw a
beautiful butterfly.

> My block is nice. The smell is nice. I have fun on my
> block. I play most of the time with a good girl friend. I
> like to eat rice and beans. I like to be with my mother. I
> like trips. I like to go to school. I like to sleep until eight
> o'clock in the morning. I like to talk Spanish very much
> and I like to be home. I like to love.

It was such a beautiful day for a stroll. It was pretty to see the
trees waving like an ocean at the beach. Walking is the prettiest
part of Morgie. I love to look at blue and moving clouds, do
you?

> One night David was playing "Batman" on the piano and
> everyone started fighting. We beat up all the counselors.
> And then it was time to clean up; we had this place spar-
> kling clean.

Animals love to lay in the sun
Mostly the turtle.
It loves to lay in the sun south in Florida.
Some tortoises are big as my mother.
August is the end of camp and boys and girls will be sad to
leave our wonderful camp and go back to school. School is
great for some people but most people dislike school. I like
school because if you go along with the courses you do great
but if you don't pay attention, you don't do too good.

*   *   *

108

MORGIE FIRST   Editor: Irving L. Gadfly
"An hey for houchmagandie" — Robert Burns
Friday, August 16, 1968 — Vol. 1, No. 8
Mood: Lewd   Cost: Non sense

THE SOUTH ATHOL WEAK END MORNING BUNGLE   Wuxtry Late Edition

Advertisements:
- I've got shoes. You've got shoes. All God's children got shoes. *Wear 'em!*
                                                    — The Health Center
- Be an athletic supporter! Come to the intra-staff, coed softball game!
- See tomorrow's BUNGLE for the winner of this week's "Bungler of the Week" contest!
- PHIL for PRESIDENT — Phil's mother

News:

Phil's "Frog in Every Throat" presidential campaign has ground to a halt. He has asked his delegates to throw their weight behind *Mad's* Alfred E. Newman, the "What Me Worry?" candidate.

Issue of the Day: DISCIPLINE!

Your editor helped put a pile of campers to bed last night, identifying himself graciously with the working class. From this experience several thoughts arise. Counselors have sometimes viewed the editorial line of this paper as well as the orientation of the Boston College course as one of ultra permissiveness. Although both your editor and professor have cordially declined such a label, it has managed to stick.

Last night should mark the permanent demise of the permissive illusion. Your editor strictly enforced quiet during story time, made each child stay in her own bed and dramatically punished two offenders by removing them forcefully from the scene.

109

There is nothing particularly good about permissiveness in child care. In fact it can be extremely harmful because it may be read by them as "not caring." Neither, on the other hand, is there anything to write home about in a strict approach because that can often be seen as gratuitously punitive.

We must also keep cultural factors in mind. What is seen as non-punitive in *your* home may be seen as mean and ugly in mine. We have developed this theme elsewhere. And shall do so again.

Further, we (here at the *Bungle*) tend to find the strict-permissive continuum prescriptively meaningless. There are more helpful ways of viewing things. We suggest that the dimension: child- versus adult-centered, may be such a way.

Editorially this paper has long maintained a child-centered policy. It is here, however, that we are sometimes at odds with your professor who tends occasionally to veer off into adult-centered forays. We agree nevertheless that the purpose of our camp is to help children grow into strong, self-respecting, compassionate human beings.

The role of the adult is to set expectations and challenges and to provide one model of what a child might choose to grow up to be like.

The child needs freedom to try out new roles and behaviors but at the same time he needs to see adults around him who are not afraid to assert themselves, to make reasonable demands, to protect younger and weaker people and, when there is something to be done, to say: "It is now time. Get with it!" There are other occasions when it is equally appropriate to say: "You decide." It all depends but it is *always* up to the adult to set the scene at some level, to be salient; to be somewhere, somehow in charge, ultimately responsible.

We will never know how much these kids need us and depend on us. And we will never know just how good a job we have done this summer, even those among us who may feel quite inadequate at the moment.

We're doing fine! Chin up!

— I. Gadfly (You, Jane)

Tomorrow: Moynihan versus the black family. Ryan for the defense.

Question of the week: What does "houchmagandie" mean?

Answer: Marvin Kitman*

*to *Last* week's question, dope!

*   *   *

August 25, 1969

Memorandum to: Dean Donald Donley, School of Education, Boston College

From: Dr. Robert Belenky

Many things happened this summer. No one had an easy time. No one came away unscathed. Few could honestly say that they enjoyed themselves. Many felt like quitting and a few did. But everyone learned a great deal about children and, what is far more important, about themselves.

The summer has convinced me beyond even my prior conviction that a camp can provide an exquisite setting for people interested in such fields as teaching, counseling, social work, recreation, or psychology. More so than in school, people here extend themselves far beyond what they previously supposed their limits to be.

It is only at camp that the sheep in child care can adequately be separated from the goats. It is only in such a setting that one can ever know if the strains of working closely with children and having to care for their physical, intellectual, and emotional needs is personally tolerable. Some of our staff discovered that for them it was *not* tolerable. Others found to their surprise that being responsible for children was enormously gratifying.

There is much to think about and plan for.

*   *   *

111

January 4, 1970

Lots of ideas came out of that camp experience. That fall
I wrote three separate proposals for different kinds of summer
utopias in which kids and adults, rich and poor, professors,
students, workers unemployed, and captains of industry
could all be blended in together; where learning and service
could be combined and where a life of productivity could
be united with pleasure and the arts. The following summer
I took the family to Nova Scotia in the hopes of finding a
large amount of cheap, beautiful land that we could develop
into such a community. We found a two hundred acre island
with three beaches in a warm sea. But it was sold out from
under me before I could act. Meanwhile, life spun on and
that particular fantasy was left behind.

Jim Reed came up to camp as a guest speaker. He talked
about Black Power and its history in this country, Nat
Turner, Frederick Douglass, W. E. B. Du Bois, Marcus
Garvey, and Malcolm X. Much discussion was generated and
it continued for weeks. Jim always makes his presence felt.
Some of the Playroom 81 mothers and one father came
also — but at another date — to talk about what it's like
living with welfare and housing hassles, destructive schools,
and grinding poverty. Mr. and Mrs. Searcy were there and Mrs.
Kuhn and Mrs. Paige. I like and respect Mr. Searcy but never
got to know him well. His wife ran the program, achieved
considerable recognition for it while he remained in the background, proud of her. I often wondered if her prominence
was hard for him to take. He is a very bright man. Cool.
Attracts kids like the Pied Piper. He asked what would become
of his own kids, too decently brought up ever to become
competent in street life, but too crippled by the schools,
racism, and housing project life to make it by the standards of
the American Dream.

Chapter Four

LHE MENLAL HEALLH WORKER

July 7, 1969

It's my first day of work at the Mass. Mental Health Center.
At the moment the social workers are explaining their role
to the new residents. Two men have Sigmund Freud beards.
My friend Joanne, the psychologist in my line of vision, is
paring her nails. Six heads in left hands, intent expressions.
Some eyes are closed. One man is reading. Another woman
is smoking, her thumb playing with her lips, smoke curling
from clean oval nostrils of her pale arched nose. Her cheek
hidden from view by angular yellow hair. "At first sight
thought to be a senile, demented person. . . ." "Dr. Ludden,
Dr. John Ludden . . . Miss Robino, Miss Robino. . . ." "The
problems are such that they can't properly be handled in
the hospital. . . ." "Not knowing that other agencies are
involved." "Extremely understaffed." "Thirty per cent of
social workers are leaving because of salary."

Walked to Playroom 81 down the street and through the
projects. Summer has come, despite the broken glass.
Children chase each other. Saw Barbara Searcy, Joyce
Pulley, and Dody Lewis. Walked back. My assignment will
be Jamaica Plain. Mary Scanlon is coordinator for that area.
Joanne Brabson and Joanne Schriber will both be working
there. Talked with them.

I'd like to begin with adolescent group therapy, using

trainees who eventually take over the group while I start another one. Eventually I'd like to have a free building from the BRA and create a learning center, manned by B.U. students, interns, residents, and local people. In such a center a wide spectrum of cerebral and creative activities would take place including study halls, discussion groups, meetings, arts, drama, writing, contemplating; being with investigating. . . .

I would love . . . to make movies.

* * *

July 14, 1969; Monday

Went around my assigned area, Jamaica Plain, after meeting with staff which left me at sea. Few of them go out and hang around neighborhoods. I cannot contain my own impatience and curiosity.

John Reed, a minister turned psychologist, joined me. He seems small-town midwestern. We are both anomalous in urban poor Boston.

We went searching . . . .

(The dull ache will be gone this afternoon and the tooth and its lower jaw partner replaced by two salty swill holes and more severe pains. Oh, son-of-a-bitch, I am very chicken!)

We met Mr. Eskew, who directs the Jamaica Plain Neighborhood House. Told us to wait while he set up a volleyball game. We watched the kids play, particularly David, who was graceful, strong, and good-humored. He showed himself magnificently for the girls. We strolled to the Martha Elliott Health Center to see Shu Shu Ritter, who wasn't there. Then we walked to Centre Street, out of the Bromley-Heath Project, passed a tavern with Irish men drinking and a few Puerto Rican people on the street, adolescent boys without shirts hustled the ball to each other on the basketball court in the playground. A thin drawn

114

pale mother in a faded blue-pink print dress pushed a carriage.

We entered the United Baptist Church. No one was there so we found a house, kind of for recreation and study, where we met Reverend Gasper, the Pastor, and Henry Fizer, his assistant, who is interested in youth and has an orange moustache. We tried out some ideas, the best of which would seem to be a network of small groups of teen-agers and young adults around Jamaica Plain in each of many churches, community centers, and other agencies, with co-leadership by B.U. grad students and community persons who might then become enrolled in the B.U. Special Education Program, where I now also work. They would meet with regular groups of no more than six or eight young people. These meetings might begin with self-orientation and move toward seminar-focus on out-there reality, literature, social change, even revolution. Leaders would meet similarly with me each week. Most intriguing.

Last Friday Charlie Weiss and I also walked around the neighborhood. Met Karen Wilke, a kid from last summer's camp. We were very glad to see each other and I treated her and her friend to soft drinks. Orangeade.

The project seems in terrible repair. Much broken glass. Burned-out apartments. Many, many people. Almost all black. Few haggard whites, Puerto Ricans. We saw a woman with a knife go after another woman. Drunk man with gold teeth tried to stand between. Neighbors mostly jeered. We averted our glance, kept stupidly walking.

September 9, 1969
Working with the Boston University students, and I am under the impression that we are already moving too quickly. Students want to start two schools, one around Nick's place and the other in the Bromley-Heath Housing Project.

There are all sorts of questions that must be raised about

115

how one gains entré into a community. Perhaps the best way is to offer a needed service and at the same time set one's sights on something beyond.

The students might enter as tutors, providing marginal help. But in so doing they would become part of the neighborhood and, after gaining respect, learn to give more.

I wonder if my own role might be different from that of the students. Could I focus on interpersonal problem discussions while the students concentrate on learning? Group therapy and group learning might ultimately fuse to provide a new entity perhaps encased in new institutions. Let's keep thinking.

What is Nick's place?

September 16, 1969

Nick Moccia's place is the biggest gossip topic in Jamaica Plain. People think he's a pimp, a pusher, a Fagin. I think he plays it straight but with generous doses of sentiment and well-advertised love. Very maternal but masculine. Concerned, sometimes worried, generous, and proud of the kid's successes. They try in the worst way to please him. Barbara helps a lot and they love her, too.

In July when I first started work in Jamaica Plain I first heard of Nick. The TYF* used his storefront as headquarters then. TYF is a kind of new left group with a manifesto demanding an end to police harassment and things of that sort. As one can well imagine this alone got them labeled beyond the pale by the police and the good citizens of the community. And added to this was the fact that the roughest kids in the neighborhood hung around Nick's and that boys and girls slept there all night long.

They had rules. "No hanging or stealing on or near the premises." "No open intercourse." "Eat your meals at home

*Tactical Youth Force

116

if possible." "Respect all adults." "Police not welcome without a warrant." And others. It was lovable, wild, cavalier, and wonderfully irresponsible by U.S. government-inspected standards.

The room was still dark even though it was almost eleven. Jimmy Jones was the first to wake up. He stretched and said, "Good morning, world," and reached toward the ceiling with his right elbow and then his left and then he shadowboxed a bit on his way to the sink. Nick woke up messy and unshaven with yellow sleep engraved in his face and sour caked morning mouth. He too stretched, greeted me vaguely. Stripped to the waist, tattooed, sideburns and thick black hair. Late thirties, I should judge. A tough guy. His bellbottomed jeans did not look so much fashionable as an expected part of the general picture of a pirate going off to sea.

The sentiment was hard to take at first. And the constant outward manifestations of love and affection. Taking kids into his arms and telling them that they're beautiful!

September 28, 1969
It seems to me that even the most enlightened of agencies tend to be much too oriented to agencies. They also have serious commitments to meetings. Often tedious, redundant, and probably no more than a fulfillment of mindless duty. The real heroes of our time are those who stand with kids on street corners and three a.m. alleyways. I'm thinking of Art Eskew, Nick, and now there's Dick. Dick Beede. Such people are very threatening to agencies.

Dick Beede is twenty-six or so but looks older. Maybe middle thirties. His street looks, I think, and his quick, mercurial intelligence make the man an object of at least casual adult suspicion. He has a large following of kids—maybe a couple of hundred. People say he lures them with drugs. I don't know. His manner is affirmative yet with a

lurking feel of dependency evoking pity. The kids seem
to respect him. Like others I've met recently, he wants
to prevent kids from having to go through what he did. He
is idealistic, I think, but shrewd, rational, suspicious, and
businesslike.

Nick comes on like an ample Italian mama, fiercely
dedicated to her children, and proud, boastful of their
successes. The kids love him, call him "Daddy" and kiss
him affectionately. He is sentimental, loving, and luxuriates
in their love as they in his.

Dick has attracted an older group, tougher, with more
drug experience. Dick is not at all sentimental and, if
anything, comes on like a gang leader.

Maybe I exaggerate the differences because in a way the
two men are remarkably similar and each seems to attribute
to the other his own weaknesses.

The hospital sometimes raises questions about my working
with these men because we are so uncertain of their motives.
They have no agency sponsorship and receive no salary.
Hence no status. But they attract kids and it seems to me
that that should be enough to warrant our interest and help.

*   *   *

Doc: Nick, could you just say what you're trying to do.
       What's the point of this?

Nick: Does there have to be a point? I don't know. Every-
       body does something. I'm not sure. I don't deny
       that a lot of it has probably to do with my own
       guilt feeling, loneliness when my wife left me.
       Maybe it's just native instinct in me. Most
       Italians I know are usually a little bit concerned
       about their children. I have three small ones, you
       know. I'm not there with them.

Kid: Yeah, Nick is like a father to me. My father's nothing

118

but a bum. That's why I like Nick. He always tries
to get you out of trouble. You don't lie to Nick.
If you do wrong, you do wrong.

Nick: When I first started it was in the home, in the
apartment that I had. It was a different concept
than I have now. I was much more naïve and
idealistic than I am today. A year in the strip makes
a big difference. The strip is Lamartine Street to
Washington Street, from the Bromley-Heath Project
to Forest Hills. That's the strip. I've named it the
strip. As far as I'm concerned it's the dope center,
the heartache center, the unwanted-kid center,
the unwanted-home center; that's the strip for
everything society's against or trying to put down.
I think half the crime from this area comes out of
the strip. "Criminals." They got the name and
they'll have the game. Because they know nothing
else.

Kid: There's nothing to do in your own house. You don't
feel like going to one of your friends' houses. So
you just drop in here.

Nick: I hadn't had any goals in mind when I started. It was
just to give the kids a place. It was just a place
where the kids could go and do their own thing and
not be bothered. And also it gave them, it gave *me*
a sense of belonging to something. It was just to
have a club, just a place for the kids to go . . .
until people started to rebuff me. People were
against kids having a place to go. I resented people
interfering with the kids when the kids weren't
doing anything. I started to talk with the kids, to
rap with them. A lot of them started to come for
different reasons. Many because they have no real
folks and this was a home to them. I was sort of
an orphan, too, you know, Doc. I felt that the

119

kids were a little special part of me. You know,
if there was some way I could have them per-
manently, I would love to have them.

You know how Janie* says, "Nick, cuddle up
right close. You're our family and that's why we
like to stay here. We don't go home because there's
nothing for us and we know it. In here, even if it's
dirty and it's messy at least it's home and *you're*
here." I really felt kind of nice.

Kid: Nick really started this thing. It started in the yellow
house. Nick moved in the yellow house over there
and the kids started coming around and visit him
and we all started going down there, and these
people downstairs, the landlords, started calling
the cops and Nick didn't want to get rid of the
kids 'cause he really thought we could start something. It started with the truck. Nick was a
contractor and making big money. He had some
kids work for him in Charlestown. Nick built
nightclubs. When the job was over, Nick had to let
the kids go. The kids got mad and stole his truck.
Nick went out and found out who they were and
invited them up to his room to play cards and
talk. Kids used to go up there all the time. There
were fishing trips and stuff like that. He really
spent a lot of money on us. He still does. People
started calling up. And he went to court for us
kids. Nick finally got kicked out. He didn't want
to leave us out in the street to steal cars anymore
so he opened up the club on Green Street. That
was this summer. Trips every weekend. That place
got burned out and then this place was open and
we moved in but we didn't have no furniture.
We took some good furniture from abandoned
houses and windows and everything for this place.
Fixed it up. Took us about three months to

120

really fix this place up, paint it and everything.
Now look at it. Now look at it. A shambles. That's
because when Dick Beede's Club, the Boylston
Club, got burned out the kids hung around here.

Nick: I've rapped to them by the hour when they've
been speeding or tripping and I've come to know
them a little better as people and not just wayward
kids that have records or kids that are dope addicts.
Just people. I kind of dig these kids. They're a
bunch of bastards. They screw you out of anything.
They try to beat you out of the jukebox and
they wreck the walls and break the windows and
sneak booze in. The kids all know that I won't
fink to the cops. They know that if they're in
trouble I'll take care of them. They all know
that if they run away from jail they can come
here and I'll take care of them. I'll also try to get
them to go back, but if they don't want to, I
won't force them.

Kid: This club has really gotten all kinds of kids. All the
kids from all different areas come around. One
kid from down that corner will be afraid to go
up that corner and that kid from that corner will
be afraid down there. You know, here all the
kids get together. All your friends come down
here. When somebody is chasing you the best
thing to do is run back here. Get in trouble,
Nick will always help you out. And we stick
together. When Johnny Smith* was on the run
and some kids set on him down the street, the
whole club chased them down the street. Three
nights in a row the whole club was down looking
for the kids and we weren't fooling around
either. Even us little kids went down there.

Nick: Sometimes I really don't understand why they

121

want to come here. It's cold. There's no heat, dirty, every one of them that hangs around here long enough ends up with a cold but they constantly come and they fight with me. But when they're in trouble, they run here first. When they find somebody else in trouble they bring him here. And as many times as they threaten to shoot me, kill me, knife me, stab me, they still come back. Whether or not I'm doing right by the kids and whether or not I'm on an ego trip, I'm not sure. But I'm afraid of the possibility that this *might* happen to me—being able to control the kids' minds and being able to get them to do what I want them to do on whim or just on words. I'm scared of it, and because of it, I'm really cautious.

Jimmy Jones is my conscience. I need him, I know. I am an adult. I am not a kid. I cannot be a kid. I cannot regress. I must be what I am. To assume something that I'm not would only be playing a role. I think that eventually the kids would get tired of that. Like Jimmy, I found that every time I'm at fault or I fail, he's very angry and becomes quite upset and wants to destroy me and what I've tried to build. He does not and will not accept the fact that I am just a human being. I've tried to explain to him that I'm only a human being with a human being's failings and that since no one is really helping me I will make a lot of mistakes. But he won't accept it.

Many a time I think kids have laughed and joked because I woke up in the morning in those king-sized beds with maybe three or four girls in bed with me. I'd be tired coming home from work and just flopped in the nearest bed. And slept. It would look funny but I was there to sleep. I'll admit that I have, well, I wouldn't say taken advantage of the social workers that come down here, but I've slept with them. All of them. On our first trip last summer I hit two the same night. But I don't pay any attention to that. They're old enough and I didn't have any compulsions about taking them. They made it obvious and I accepted it. I'm a male. I'm a full male and there's no denying that. I like to enjoy the fruits of what God gave us, and believe me that's not little kids. Anybody who's spent the night here will tell you. I don't fool around with children.

As far as the dope pushers. They're kids. They're accepted as long as they don't deal in the club and as long as they don't give to the young kids. A couple of dope pushers started the rumor that I push drugs here in order to get me in trouble with the adult community. As you know, I'm against dope in any form. I've come to be a little bit more tolerant of it recently only because I realize now the older kids are going to take it whether I holler or not. But I'm against any kid getting it and I know that the pushers do come into the club with it. But I try to stop them. The pushers started the rumor originally because I stopped all of the kids that came to my house from taking dope. For a period of three months not one of them touched dope. That hurt the pushers.

I've felt that if I could start a business. . . . I know construction and a lot of the kids have worked in it. I'd like to get a business started with government help where these kids would get the minimum wage paid by the company. The

government could pay the difference while
they're learning. I'd hire a few skilled laborers or
skilled carpenters to work for 'em. These kids
would go with the skilled laborers and work. A
lot of these kids work six or seven weeks. Then
somebody finds out that they have a bad record
and they're asked to leave or resign or get
thrown out or are fired.

I'd also like to see a creative workshop get off
the ground.

Another thing that I'd be very much interested
in is a learning center. A lot of kids indirectly are
always talking about how they wish they hadn't
quit school but they can never go back. Now, a
dropout school — like a street academy — is the
perfect answer.

Doc: Hey, if they had the school thing here, would you go?
Kid: No. Like I was in the Bowditch School, right? Like I
       was—stupid! You know. I just didn't want to do
       this and do that. Getting the stick in there, too.
       Just promoted me to pass me on. I went to the
       seventh grade in the Curley School. I was never *in*
       school. I used to hook like every other day. They
       kept me back in seventh grade. I turned fifteen.
       I was the biggest one in the class. I just never went
       to school. All my marks were bad. So they decided
       to put me in a work-study program and they gave
       me a double promotion to the ninth grade. I
       couldn't do ninth-grade work at all. So then I did
       about two or three months in the work-study—may-
       be four months—then I quit. I was fifteen years old
       and I said, "Oh, fuck. I'm quitting this shit. I
       can't stand it!" I know one thing. I ain't gonna get
       my license 'cause I know I can't go down to the
       registry and read the form to fill out my thing.
       It's that bad. I can't do shit.

124

Doc: Do you think of yourself as stupid?

Kid: I don't know. I just don't want to learn. When I go for a job, I get the form and bring it home. Man. My mother fills it out for me. Then I bring it back. I was in the ninth grade, right? And it was just before graduation. I didn't graduate but my picture was in the book. And all the teachers come to me, "Did you graduate?" "Yeh. Yeh. See. My picture's in the book."

Doc: One of the reasons I brought this school business up is because Barbara Epstein is talking about setting up a school down here. Now Barbara is a teacher. She worked at the Curley last year.

Kid: She ain't a teacher no more. She's like a big sister. You don't have to call her Miss Epstein anymore. She tries to convince the kids not to take dope and stuff like that. No, Barbara's a really nice woman. She's not like a teacher. She tries to help the kids out when they do wrong. She sometimes helps them with their school lessons.

Doc: What would a school down here be like?

Kid: I don't think it would work out. You know, the kids, they tore the walls out here, right? There's no reason why they couldn't tear the school up.

Doc: Do you think there could be a school that could also be an interesting place to go to?

Kid: Yeh, if Miss Epstein was teaching, it would be. Yeah, if there was a teacher in every school like Miss Epstein, wow!

*　　*　　*

Notes from the Charles Street Jail — "No Hassle"

January 9, 1970; Dick Beede
I think that problems of mass social unrest and revolt cannot

125

be remedied overnight. It is a serious attempt by the youth to foment an internal revolution. It is a revolution geared toward forcing the adult community into a state of full awareness of what is going in on this world. I think that adults have grown accustomed to national and world strife and have been inclined to minimize the problems of their own lives in relation to their communities and families. It is almost as if a national social plague has diseased this country.

The major problems existing on a local level appear to be assault and battery, breaking and entering, car thefts, and such common "high" crimes as liquor and hard and soft dope. Although these are offenses of a diverse nature, they are all committed basically for the same reason: the kids are screaming for some form of recognition. They get it by being seen doing these things. They want to be associated with outstanding acts merely to bring the light of recognition on themselves. "I, John Smith, am alive. See me." Beyond this, delinquent acts bring them into contact with other youths with basically the same emotional needs. Hence "The Brotherhood" is formed.

The remedy I have found is simple. It is an attitude of absolute understanding and acceptance: "No matter what you say I can't be shocked." I call it the "no hassle" system. If I see a kid all drunked up or doped up or riding a stolen car, I don't hassle him because he is exercising an inner need to revolt. I'm not saying that I necessarily condone these acts of social rebellion. I am simply saying that I recognize them as such and don't try to correct what the kid is doing. I also try to be there first to help the kid when the hard times come. I've found that when using this system the kid may repeat these crimes again but with less and less frequency.

It seems that once they have found an adult they can relate to, they begin to stop messing around because they all have a basic desire to be approved of. If they think you're going to be disappointed, they become disappointed with themselves and they discover the remedy themselves. When I say you become disappointed, I mean just that. Not angry, mad, hateful, judgmental—just disappointed.

I know that my system works. It worked with me when I was a kid. Kids accept my form of dealing with them, remembering that I am a common layman, not educated by the masters of sociological construction. I've reacted as my nature allowed and I've become extremely popular in youthful circles and extremely *un*popular in adult ones. Some adults think that I encourage kids to act the way they do but that is not so. I am unpopular because I am completely frank when talking to adults about kids. I can't see standing around talking bullshit: "Oh, what will people say if we do it that way?" To *hell* with what people say! The kid needs help. Let's help him!

One thing I have to say about my method is that it is sure to meet with some of the most violent criticism available. For example, I try to make it a point *not* to meet the parents or at least to run into them as little as possible. I feel that once you've met them, you begin to develop a certain responsibility to them that could later conflict with the system of "no hassle." I like to leave the parental scene to the social worker sitting in his office.

The old method was: "Kick kids in the ass and they'll keep quiet." This will no longer work. Kids have found their unity in one another. They no longer have to keep quiet and they know it. By banding together, the youth are using the only means in their power to make their needs known. Let's face it. Can a young man or woman under voting age walk up to an established authority in this country and be heard by any one? Would they be taken

127

seriously? Of course not! Adults sit on their fat, content asses and comment on the destruction the kids are causing but neither deal with nor understand the reasons.

Adults are running amuck, making ignorant, wild, and libelous statements about the intent of the youth.

Adults should wake up and get involved personally with youth. If young people could get a "no hassle" involvement from adults it might return this society back to the time when a kid was proud to be seen with his family. Something to think about!

* * *

It is very difficult to know how and where to stand with respect to the community and the kids in particular. I want in a way to be absolutely at one with them the way Nick is—and Dick, too—devoted and loving but yet retaining earned respect; a nuturant mentor, an adult. But I do not have the time, nor really do I have the interest. Twenty-four hours a day and seven days a week. Everything. Nick's heaven and his hell. His prison. I think perhaps ungenerously that he is doing penance. And so is Dick. It is a religious mission, and perhaps one of them is the true God or His messenger. The other may be Satan. (That would, of course, be Dick Beede who has bright red hair and was once one of Nick's chief lieutenants. They had a squabble and Dick left to set up his kingdom of the damned down the street.) But I am not at all made of apocryphal stuff. I am a marginal man. A tourist. Leopold Bloom.

So I wander along the edge. Afraid to get involved but wishing to be of use. Is there a role? I want to hear their problems and make everyone feel better. Of course, that's bullshit but it *is* the logic of my position.

What *can* I do?

1. I'm about to open a satellite center with the collaboration of Mrs. Helene Harris from the Community Leadership Council. (Try not to attend to the details.) There we will run a "problem-solving clinic." The hospital objects to my offering "therapy," which is just as well since I'm not a true believer. Adolescents (parents, too?) will be welcome to come in and discuss any sort of problem with an objective listener and receive direct reality help or emotional support.

2. We will also have weekly meetings with people like Dick and Nick and Art Eskew (I haven't talked about him yet because I know him only slightly but I think he's a most interesting man). These meetings will essentially be case conferences in which we will study how we deal with children. Maybe course credit can forthcome. VerVaist?

3. I'll wander around in the mornings and go to court as an advocate.

4. I'll help kids who are thrown out of school.

5. I'll help the school deal mercifully with kids who hook.

6. I'll talk with parents and . . . help?

7. I'll get meetings going about funding and whip together a good proposal for all of Jamaica Plain's youth.

8. I'll get lots of students who can help do all of the above.

9. I'll reform the Massachusetts Mental Health Center and Boston University.

10. I'll go home exhausted, having accomplished nothing and without even the ego-trip

129

titillation fondly enjoyed by some of my
comrades . . . .

*   *   *

November 19, 1969

The other day we had a meeting of youth workers from
Jamaica Plain in the kitchen of the rectory house of the
United Baptist Church. Vivian Thompson made the
spaghetti. John Leary brought a couple of bottles of wine
and I bought instant coffee at the little Puerto Rican
grocery store around the corner on Centre Street. Nick
said that nobody does a goddamned thing except go to
meetings. We have soft jobs while *he* works twenty-four
hours a day seven days a week and he's fucking tired.
Nobody does anything, not even you, Doc. There are
ways to get this thing funded, Nick, but you've got to be
more together. Didn't we tell you (how many times?) to
form a board of directors, trustees, invent bylaws, pull
in a kindly free lawyer, and get yourself incorporated as a
tax-deductible, charitable, educational institution? We are
doing that, we are working on it. Model cities will come
through with something and then we can write a proposal.
Even if not incorporated, can't we use some already-existing
organization as a conduit, an umbrella, or whatever? Pipe
the funds through them? We can give inspirational talks
to suburban church groups. It is complicated but has
happened for worse ideas. It takes knowhow and time.
Can't we form a committee of hustlers to get on this?
But Nick wants a *family*. And kids need one. Incorporation
may kill it. Nick might become, instead, a public
institution with hundreds of kids. Heaven forfend! Any
funding strategy would have to preserve the littleness of
little groups.

*   *   *

In the Car: Doc, Kevin, and Jimmy

November 21, 1969

Doc: See, Kevin. If you take that course in funding, you'll learn how to get bread to support the club.

Jimmy: *I* know how to get bread. I've been getting it all my life.

Doc: I know, but I mean *legitimately*.

Jimmy: I can do it so people can't take me to court but they still get screwed.

Doc: You mean some kind of hustling racket or something like that?

Jimmy: Yeah. I do a little hustling. Shit, why not? I been a politician all my life.

Doc: Yeah, but you can't. . . . I mean could you keep the club supplied through hustling. I mean like with a hundred thousand dollars a year?

Jimmy: Um hm!

Doc: A budget for a very small school is like a hundred thousand a year. Could you pull in that kind of money by hustling? I don't think so.

Jimmy: Me and two kids I know could.

Doc: That would take a lot of time.

Kevin: At this corner's perfect, Doc.

Jimmy: You gotta take a right, anyway.

Doc: Hum?

Jimmy: We're taking a right, anyway.

Doc: What?

Jimmy: What? Huh? What did I say? How-much-does-it cost-ya?

Doc: How much does what cost?

Jimmy: To die.

Doc: Oh, to die.

Jimmy: I said, "To die."

Doc: You said, "To die."

Jimmy: I said you gotta concentrate on your driving.

131

Don't listen to me. Ha Ha ha ha.

Doc: Jimmy, I don't know what you're talking about.

Jimmy: I said, "WE'VE GOT TO TAKE A RIGHT, ANY-
WAY."

Doc: Oh, a *right*. Very good.

Kevin: What are we talking about dying for? I get off here.

Jimmy: No (pointing to some old ladies), *they're* talking
about dying. They're worrying about it. They
wish they were us. Look at them. *Envious!* And
this kid (teen-ager with a marked limp) is worrying
'cause he's got a peg leg. He's singing to himself.
He's trying to be happy but he's not. Right?

Doc: You're probably right.

Kevin: You a psychiatrist?

Jimmy: In my own unconventional way. Secretly. Oh, well.

Doc: He *is* a psychiatrist!

Jimmy: I used to make anywhere from a hundred to three
hundred dollars a night stealing, right? Sometimes
a thousand dollars a night, right? If I stole a
hundred dollars every night for one year I'd have
three hundred and fifty-two thousand dollars. . . .

Doc: But eventually you'd get busted.

Kevin: So long, Doc. Thanks for everything.

Jimmy: Um hm. But all I'd have to do is each time make
the odds better.

Doc: See you, Kevin.

Kevin: Yeh.

Jimmy: Good-bye.

Doc: Yeh but you know instead of robbing banks and stuff
like that; instead of doing that. . . .

Jimmy: Hi, beautiful! Hi, girl! I like girls, you know that?

Doc: I noticed that.

Jimmy: Yeh, they're nice.

*   *   *

Nick and the Establishment, Part I

December 1969

They came in at four o'clock in the morning, banged on the door. I opened it up. I never seen so many of them, Doc. All the way around—flashlights. I said, "Hey, take that flashlight out of my face!"

He says, "Hey, don't get fresh."

I said, "This is my house. If you want a light, ask me. I'll turn one on."

They said, "We're looking for a guy who was in an accident. He tried to run a cop over."

I said, "Oh, I don't know anything about it. I was asleep."

He says, "Well, who came in?"

I said, "How do I know? I was asleep!"

"Don't get fresh," he said.

I said, "Goddamit, you come into my house. You accuse me of having a kid in here while I'm sleeping and then you tell me I'm getting fresh. *You're* getting fresh!"

He started screaming.

"Lower your voice," I said. "I'm right *here*."

I said, "Now if you people want, you're welcome to look around but don't tell me something I don't know anything about."

"Who are you looking for anyway?" I asked.

They told me and I got *bull*shit. I said it wasn't him because he was shooting pool here and he went right home and went to bed. They told me I didn't know what I was talking about.

I said, "All right then, let's go down to his house and see if he's sleeping."

Then they tried to tell me that he had ample time to go home and go to bed.

I says, "Then what are you coming *here* for?"

* * *

Nick and the Establishment, Part II

December 1969

The State Department of Public Works said that they're going to take me out of here today so that the inner belt highway can come through. The state inspector came down at four o'clock last night and told me. It was all I could do to stop the kids from dismantling the crane. The man got afraid because the kids told him they'd burn the crane last night so he said he was going to take another house first and leave us time—until this afternoon.

Doc: Why did you do that?

Kid: We just did it for Nick so he'd have a place to live so he wouldn't have to sleep on the pool table.

Doc: What are you going to do when they come and try to take it today?

Kid: I'm going to tell them they can kiss my _____ 'cause they ain't taking it!

Kid: Look what we did here! We did the whole upstairs—made a teen nightclub out of it. We got the pool table and the jukebox and we cleaned out this place and we had that spaghetti dinner and we even got that apartment next door to make a learning center in. Nick wouldn't let us in unless we cleaned it. I think we should have it, man. I worked hard on this place.

Official: Nick, we came to get you out of the premises!

Nick: Do you have a release?

Official: Not for you, 'cause you're a squatter, Nick.

Nick: I was given a verbal promise.

Official: You've got nothing at all in writing? Better go!

Nick: I had an *oral agreement!* Isn't that good enough among men today?

Official: I don't know, Nick. This is The State. This is a State Building and we want you out!

Nick: How come the mayor's office gave us a few hundred

dollars to fix the place up if they want us out of
here? Oh, shit. It just seems to be one thing after
another, one crisis after another. I never seem to
get out of one and there's another one.

Kid: I'm here because this place is keeping us off the
streets. I like it. I think Nick's a great guy. He's
given his life for us kids.

Kid: He helped us kids stay off the corner. He helped us
build this place and they ain't taking it down.

*   *   *

Until last week's storm you could tell where Nick's place
was because there was no snow on that square patch of land.
Now the snow covers everything.

*   *   *

The White Doctor's Burden

December 1, 1969

The issue of medical responsibility came up in a staff meeting
yesterday. Viewed by the hospital, I suspect that just about
everyone we work with in the field is a patient—unless he's a
physician—because each of us is a physician (or an ancillary
physician because our ultimate boss is a physician and we are
extensions of him).

We are physician-tools.

The physician in charge is concerned that we function
properly, for if the patient dies (or, more likely, does something which meets with public disfavor), he, the physician,
can be blamed by other physicians.

Medical training—how to set a broken tibia, what to
prescribe for the measles—is training for operations on the
body politic. The chief physician is the chief politician.

(It all gets mixed up.)

135

Clear, however, is that the concept of medical responsibility leads to concern with control and also that the
hospital's hierarchical design is neatly suited to house-control
mechanisms. Responsible for the patient, everyone is
accountable to the next man up. Everyone is supervised.
Independent decision-making is possible only when the
values of the system have demonstrably been internalized.

Medical training is bureaucracy training.

Doctors make good bureaucrats. They *should* be in charge.
Better respected than just any Joe Blow.

The M.D. is a guarantee.

Up doctors.

Folk Medicine!

December 12, 1969; Dr. Beede Reflects

How did I, a twenty-six year old man of relative intelligence,
wind up here, in the situation I'm in and in the area I'm in?

Jamaica Plain is not an entirely new area to me. I, at the
age of approximately twelve to fourteen years of age, for
various reasons too long to discuss here, wound up hanging
around in the Heath Street Housing Project. I can say that
I have been influenced in later life by my time spent there.
This experience, coupled with the rest of my juvenile tramp-
ings, has been a great aid in developing the ability I have
to communicate with the kids of this area at present.

I have in the far and recent past been in communication
with the guys that I associated with when I was in this area
as a youth. Most of these people have made some pretty
wild reputations for themselves since then and, coupled
with mine, I can honestly state that this is what gives me so
much command here. However, it is not the original appeal
I had that drew the kids I have now.

Where do I work? Well, all I can say is along the railroad
tracks or in the playground or three or four a. m. any summer
morn or some drop-in center or just anywhere. I have no

office and no one to answer to but my conscience. With this type of official backing I've become the "Ideal Youth Worker" to many kids. And an ogre of sorts to organized youth groups in the area who have not been able to make even a passing contact (meaningful) with the kids in the areas mentioned. By the term "groups" I mean the city- or state-backed organizations staffed by workers who are inexperienced in actual on-the-street contact and the real hardships that these youth are experiencing personally.

The area where I work has for many years held the honor of being the hardest-core area of Jamaica Plain and it appears that they are working to retain this title. The constant repetition of crimes, such as outstanding auto thefts, enormous damage by arson, to say little about the B and E's and assaults and the almost maniacal universal desire and use of weapons, the personal chronic need to carry and possess firearms and the least of desired weapons, a knife.

* * *

January 5, 1970

I simply cannot communicate to you how insane it is. Insanity compounded a thousandfold. We were out of town for a three-day New Year's ski weekend. Returned to find Jamaica Plain totally different. Unbelievable.

Dick Beede got busted on New Year's eve for shooting a man at a party. The man, the kids say, came downstairs to say that Dick and the kids were making too much noise. Dick, they say, was drunk, took down his .22, and shot him. The man is on the danger list at the Peter Bent Brigham hospital. Dick is in the Charles Street Jail. I called the warden. I will visit Dick on Friday.

How I discovered what happened: I drove down Lamartine Street to find Dick to tell him that I wanted a long interview with him for the book. Knocked at his door.

137

A dog barked inside. No one came. I said, "Dick. Dick Beede. Are you there?" I tried the knob. The door opened. Inside everything was a mess. I thought, "What a slob." Then it occurred to me that it was purposely wrecked. The dog whined. When I reached out for him, he hid under the sofa. I drove away and met one of the kids. I gave him a ride home. He told me the story. Later I got a kid to take care of the dog, who might have starved to death. It seemed lame, too.

It was funny that the kids that we met at Aram's Store and Papa Gino's Pizzeria did not seem overly sad. They talked about everything else. When we asked them what they intended to do about Dick, they said things like:

> "What's to do? God himself couldn't do anything for him now."
>
> "How can *I* do anything? If I show my face around, I'll get busted, too. You know my record, Doc?"
>
> "They put him on $25,000 bail. Man, they're going to throw the book at him."
>
> "He was a good guy but kind of crazy, you know."
>
> "So? He got busted. So?"

When we asked about Nick, it seemed that everybody was down on him. Comments like:

> "I couldn't take that guy any longer, I'm glad it happened."
>
> "He just *used* us kids. Charged two dollars a month, and then the jukebox and the pool table brought in maybe forty dollars a night."
>
> "It was Nick, Nick, Nick."
>
> "So? Now we hang out at Aram's, Papa Gino's, and the bowling alley. We only went to Nick's because it was warm."
>
> "I don't need *anybody*. I just broke up with my boy friend. I feel like a new woman."

It was hard to understand. In part they were expressing

honest thoughts that they had expressed before in other ways. In part they were giving voice to their disappointment and impotence translated into anger. They were rejecting those who had failed them. . . crushed by the steamroller.

*　*　*

January 9, 1970

I spent the morning in the Charles Street Jail talking with Dick Beede. Heavy, iron-barred doors rolled open and shut. I walked down the metal corridors straight ahead up the stairs and came to a door that didn't open by itself. I peeked through the hole made for that purpose and saw quite a different scene. Symmetrical stairs at the other side of a large open area. The stairs, like fire escapes in old school buildings, seemed to lead up to nothing in particular. There were men walking silently up and down. The jailer finally came with his key and I entered. Saw Dick after a while. I reproached him. "You poor damned jerk." He evaded the mood. "Let's talk," he said guiltlessly. He says he shot the guy in a kind of self-defense after having been tabbed with acid. It may be so.

*　*　*

Paul ("Hoss") Harding and His Brother, Phil – Bikies Both – Plan a Learning Drop-In Center

Hoss:　I'd like to see programs like arts and crafts, maybe open a mod shop after a while.

Phil:　You could get a pool table in there, a pinball machine, a jukebox, and put a lock on there so the kids can't break into it.

Hoss:　The kids won't break in. 'Cause this will be *their* club. *We* don't break *our* pool table and *our* jukebox. I'm going to try to run this club like our

139

club is. Our club has got a lot of rules. If someone
says we shouldn't have anyone smoking dope in
the club anymore, the secretary says, "Want to
make it a rule?" He'll have us raise our hands.
"Who wants smoke and who doesn't?" If the guy
who don't want smoke wins, it's another rule.
Like now we have about thirty-eight rules. We
overdo it, though. To me, it isn't even a real
motorcycle club anymore. It's like a *sissy's* motorcycle club. There's always some angler: "I ain't
paying *this* fine!" If a Devil's Disciple ever said
that, they'd throw him right out. We've got too
many rules. Every time you get rid of one, someone brings in another one.

Phil: You can have a room with paint in it, big sheets of
paper, thumbtacks, and all that. If someone wants
to get high, he can go in there and paint. If four
or five couples want to, they can go in there and
draw. But say a kid goes in the paint room and he
writes "Fuck You" on the wall, that's all right.
You tell him, "Write it but take it off after."
Say someone breaks open the jukebox—kick him
out! If he wants to come back in, let him pay ten
dollars to repair it.

Hoss: You could start a car club if they all had licenses.
You could teach them things about cars — how
to build racing cars. I've got a bike out the backyard—it's a legal bike, an old one. But it's a nice
bike. It runs. I could take that apart and show
them certain things.

Phil: Then they'd all want to go out and steal motorcycles
and run around in them. Right there you'd have a
motorcycle club! Ha ha ha!

Hoss: A mod shop is the thing. That would be good. Give
them something to do. They could make things and

140

sell them in the store. Leather wallets and stuff. Girls could make dresses. All of the kids aren't going to get a chance to work in the shop. You just pick the good ones, the guys who cooperate and don't go around wrecking the club. Those who respect the club. After a while the store's going to bring in money and we can open up another store. The kids will know it. They'll try to be next in line for this next store. They'll all be fighting to be the best one. The younger ones in particular.

Phil: There's going to be no dope in the club. If the kids want to get high, that's *their* thing. They can do it outside. Same thing in our club. Same thing was true at Nick's.

Hoss: I'd want the kids to see me as Nick's helper if I ran the place. Because it's still Nick's club. Kids will always say it's Nick's club no matter who's running it. This time it will be legal. And we won't get thrown out.

* * *

Movie Review: "Man, That Was a Bad Trip"
I was talking to Phil last week. He had a leather vest, and his colors were on his back. His hair was long and he wore sideburns. He told me about his life and it reminded me of the movie I had recently seen, *Easy Rider.* I said, "Hey, did you see *Easy Rider?*"

"Oh, man, that was a *bad* trip," he said.

He told the following story:

He and thirty bikies and their girl friends went to see the movie together. They wore their colors, boots, jackets, long hair, beards, shades, etc. Entered the elite art theater where it was playing and sat right in the middle of the audience en masse. They heard it was about acid so they brought acid

141

with them and before the flick began they passed around the tabs. Soon everyone was freaked out.

"Oh, man, we really grooved on that flick! Like riding through those mountains and the beautiful scenery and the hippy community and swimming nude with the broads and when they took that acid trip we were right there with them freaking out on the beautiful colors and things. We were right in there with them. They and us were the same."

Here he became visibly agitated but continued.

"Then the ending. The crackers drive by and this cat screams at Billy 'Hey, freak, go get a haircut!' And Billy gives him the finger. I said to myself, 'Yeh, *right on*!' I was into Billy. But then the fucking bastard takes out his shotgun and blows Billy's head off and the bike goes *plffflt* into the dirt. I mean it was like everything was gone. I went crazy. I couldn't take it. So I stood up in the theater and I shook both fists at that fucking cracker and I screamed: *'You motherfucker!'* The crackers turn around and come back and blow off Captain America's head. That was too much. I stood up again and jumped over a couple of seats and I screamed *'You motherfuckerrrr!!!!'* Then the lights came on. We all were *down.* Really down. We walked out of the theater like this together, heads down, slumped, looking worried, and I mean so uptight if anybody came up to me to ask the time I would have turned around and laid him flat. I was like that for days. The rest of the audience looked at us out of the corners of their eyes and they kept a lot of space between them and us. We were like out of the flick."

*   *   *

"Trying Ain't Enough"

Group Therapy, Newton High School: Years Ago.
Jack: I thought the moon shot on television last night
        was interesting.

142

Luther*:   What was interesting about it?

Jack: I just liked to watch it, that's all.

Luther: For what? I mean, what the fuck's that gonna do? What good is it gonna do anybody?

Jack: Well, I think it's interesting.

Luther: *Why* was it interesting?

Jack: I think I have a sense of adventure, I mean I'd like to know. I'd just like to find out about things. I mean is there life on other planets? Doesn't that ever bother you?

Luther: Okay, say there's no life on other planets. So what? So, okay, say there is. What good is it gonna do you? Are you gonna marry one?

Jack: Well, I have faith in the human race. It's a sense of adventure. A sense of accomplishment. If somebody does it, then I feel part of it.

Luther: You mean because you got a prick and two legs?

Jack: Yeh, because I'm a member of the human race.

Luther: You actually believe that?

Jack: Well, maybe if a boxer wins a fight, it's just a satisfaction for himself, but when somebody does something like for outer space or science, it's not just for the person who does it. If they found a cure for cancer tomorrow, it's not just an accomplishment for one guy. It's an accomplishment for mankind.

Luther: What *good* is it gonna do to create a thing for cancer? Hey, listen, if fucking cancer don't get us, if we create such a fucking population in this world by conquering all these lethal diseases, what's there gonna be left? You're gonna have some half mad-ass Chink. He's gonna set off a few H-bombs and then we won't have so many people. We might as well not even *conquer* these diseases.

Jack: Yeh, but if we hadn't had the feeling of adventure,

143

we'd still be living in caves.

Luther: Well, what's wrong with living in caves? Hey, why the fuck is *he* up here? He's *normal*. Really, I'm serious. He's for all this horseshit, you know, about the better life and all that.

Jack: I'm not normal. I steal hubcaps.

Luther: That don't mean nothing.

Jack: We took a bumper off a state cop car one day.

Luther: That don't mean shit.

Doc: According to the school and the police he's a juvenile delinquent.

Luther: But otherwise he's the most hung-up character, really. And you are, too, Doc. This is frankly what I think of you: aside from all the noise, you and Jack are very dull.

Jack: I wouldn't mind living in a cave.

Luther: Well, okay, you have Alley Oop. He's living in a cave and every day he goes out and shoots a few saber-toothed tigers. He don't do any thinking. He just brings home the tigers to his woman, and his woman feeds him and his children, and he humps her once in a while, and they have a new child every nine months. Now that's how the human race developed. It kept developing like that and soon this same Alley Oop character — there was millions of them by now — would go to work and make his bread. He wouldn't think. He'd just go to work every day. Pretty soon there got to be so many people in cities that certain people, for their work, began thinking up new ideas. They started doing the thinking for all these people. They started making split-level houses and everything. So what the fuck's the difference between a split-level ranch house and a cave? What's the difference? You still have the same Alley Oop in it who's not doing any thinking

144

and he's just making his bread for himself and his
kiddies. What the fuck's the difference? I mean
the guys who are doing the thinking may be better
but there's not that many. I mean anybody who
says this world's fucked up and is trying to change
it in a way, you know. But if you got a character
who comes home to his ranch house every day,
kisses his wife, has supper with the kiddies, reads
the paper; the kids are put to bed and then he goes
fucks his wife and gets up every morning and goes
to work again. He doesn't do any thinking. It's
just a reflex. He drives his car sleepily through
the city and he goes to work. What the hell's the
difference between that guy and the caveman?
What the hell's the difference?

Doc: The caveman maybe had it over that guy because he
did a lot of things. He had to do some of the
thinking for himself. Maybe he didn't have to do
very much but he had to figure out how to do
things.

*   *   *

To whom are we responsible? That question haunts me. What
is a professional?

Doctors will be demonstrating for peace on the day of the
moratorium. Teachers, too. And psychologists. Lawyers. Thus
to show that on the issue of war personal convictions are
intense enough to supersede professional obligation.

Suppose, however, that a professional were more than a
specialist; a generalist in the service of humanity transcending
nation, class, and belief, more qualified of course to assist in
some areas than others.

Self-generating, self-correcting, receptive, knowledgeable,
dignified, worthy.

If this were true, the professional would then feel obligated

145

as a part of his professional duty to participate. Not:
"Although this has little to do with dentistry, it is nevertheless important." Rather: "I am a professional who knows
more about dentistry than war but nevertheless I must *as* a
professional follow the dictates of my conscience."

A professional is a moral leader; a species of priest. And
that is how he is taken whether at the moment he is so or not.

Yesterday a community leader and a psychiatrist each
asked me where I stood with regard to them. The community
leader asked what I would do if a crisis arose which would
place my allegiance to their community on the line. Would
I opt for the hospital? Would I march with the people or man
the machine guns? (An abstract and useless discussion. Too
"iffy.") Later the psychiatrist suggested that I am *always* a
representative of the institution and should constantly ask
myself: "Is this appropriate behavior for a representative of
the Mass. Mental Health Center?" He wondered if I really
thought that accompanying a youth to the police station at
midnight was appropriate behavior.

A school principal last week raised the same issue.

*   *   *

February 2, 1970
I shoot my mouth off. Some people take dope.

I asked them if there was anything they did well at Mass.
Mental Health.

I tried to get an emergency diagnostic on an eleven-year-
old kid and was told that it would take at least six months
and even then was unlikely.

The community mental health unit where I work brings
shrink service to the community but so far has little or no
interest in collaboration or in getting to know people,
making friends. My supervisor admitted that going out into
the field frightens her. Of course it does — it does me, too.

146

That's the paradox. Precisely an example of what I mean.

On the other hand, returning from the field to *this* place makes me feel like a freak. I'm out of it here.

I told them that we are a fifth-rate service.

*   *   *

February 5, 1970
Each Friday I'm holding increasingly large meetings sponsored by the Harvard Extension Course Commission *at* the hospital. It's a course, a workshop, in street work for uncredentialed youth workers, guys like Nick, Dick (until his bust), bikies, neighborhood mothers, and maybe a few cops if they show. Nick invited the local juvenile officer. The content is to design drop-in centers for Jamaica Plain Youth, using Nick's as a place to begin, even with its faults — we will all work together to make it great. Get funding and community support.

The bikies want to educate shrinks re the drug scene, so I asked the whole hospital community mental health staff to come. A few showed. None of the key people. The course and general approach are clearly in conflict with the spirit of our unit.

And the attractiveness of a slogan like "Fuck it" is increasing.

Chapter Five

Saints and Saviors

In this chapter several people speak for themselves: Jack
Cahill, Mary Wilson*, Aram Arsenian*, Scotty McGlynn, Art
Eskew, Curt Chapin, and Mildred Lau.

In his own way, each has done something to help others
make something of their lives. Each has been extraordinarily
effective in some ways and has failed in others. I think that
each has part of the answer. Collectively they represent an
approach, a way of thinking about social and personal
problems that makes sense.

* * *

Jack Cahill — Pirate King

I've been riding bikes for over twenty years. Got to meet a lot
of people. I'm not only the president of the club; I'm like a
father to fifty guys and their chicks. When they're having
problems they always come and see me. I don't use psychology like from the book. It's the psychology of living. Just
knowing people. I've lived a pretty wild, full life. I'm thirty-
eight years old and I've packed it. I've had experience in
almost anything anybody wants to talk to me about.

I know how to talk to people, to kids. I can do this because
I'm Irish and because of the life I've led. The life hasn't been
entirely what I've wanted. It's hard for me to explain this to

148

my friends. They think I'm very happy riding my bike and being in the club. I'm really free. Very free. Well, I've enjoyed it. I've loved every minute of it. But there are other things. A home, a wife, children, a family. In order for me to have some of the things I want, I've had to give up other things. But that doesn't squelch my desire for them.

To become a square and work and miss what there is in the world to see — the world is beautiful — I would have had to work every day for ten or twelve hours, come home, watch television, go to bed, worry about the kids. People who do this miss out on life. It shouldn't be that way. It should be the opposite, according to the priests. People like *me* should be missing out, but it's not happening that way. It's the people who are trying to live the righteous life who are losing.

The world is a fantastic place, and to be alive is just the greatest thing there is. Seventy-five percent of the world population is not alive today. They're dead. They are actually dead.

In our society the free way is considered to be wrong. Society demands that we live like my ex-father-in-law lives. Sublimely, quietly, within the laws of the Commonwealth and the laws of religion and other laws and customs and rules and regulations. I think this creates all the problems we have today. The immense set of rules are so oppressive that they almost drown the kids.

I'm not into material things. I never have been. I could walk around nude or in rags as long as I have transportation. I don't worry about how I'm going to pay the rent next month — it'll get paid. I have enough faith in whatever it is I believe in to know that in all my life whenever I needed money I always seemed to be able to get it. Something always seems to happen.

(Jack has a red beard that's going gray, trimmed but shaggy. He's a big man with the beginnings of a pot belly. Looks older than thirty-eight. A relaxed manner, courtly, underplayed but in charge. A thumb missing. His arm was in

149

a sling last month. Shot by the Hell's Angels. Jack has a very regal appearance.)

I guess I was a natural rebel from the time I was a kid. My father was a police chief in my hometown of Dedham. I think when someone in your family is in a position of authority you automatically become a rebel.

I went to a Catholic grammar school, then to a public high school. The change was a big one for me. I floated along through the first and second years of high school, because I'd already done all that work in grammar school. I became lazy and a little potty. I went through being kicked out, detention, and all that.

I went into the service. When I came home my father was very ill. He was a cop for forty years and always wanted me to be one so I joined the Dedham police force for about eight months, until my father died. I got away from it because I didn't really like it. From that time on I just kind of drifted around.

I've been in jail. I have a police record. I've been a drug addict. I've sold drugs. I've stolen bikes. I've made my living in various unpretentious ways. But I can do more good in certain areas than other people if I have the desire to do it. So can a lot of other people; a lot of ex-convicts who are trying to make a new life for themselves. These people could all be used. A guy that went to jail for grand larceny could be used to help other kids that are into the same bag. If he was a convicted murderer and he was released he could be used. But they *can't* be as it is now because society keeps a finger on top of them.

I've been doing drugs for a long, long, long time. When I got out of the service I got hooked on morphine and it took about a year to get myself off of it. I know a lot about drugs and I'd like to help keep kids from getting on them. I'm the president of a group we call DEPTH, which stands for Drug Experienced People to Help. We are trying to educate people about drugs, particularly kids.

150

You can't stop a kid once he's into drugs. There's no way you can talk him out of it. The only hope is trying to get to him when he's between nine and twelve. You have to rap with him for a little while and find out what he likes. When I talk to a twelve-year-old kid, believe it or not, I'm a twelve-year-old. I have a good in because most of the kids dig motorcycles. We have a pretty good club. All the kids know us.

Police and people in official capacity just can't understand that some of us, even though we might do drugs ourselves, don't necessarily want someone else to be on the same thing — particularly kids. I don't sell anything anymore. And I'm against hard drugs or addiction in any form. I have never sold hard stuff.

Drugs can be a good thing for some people and a bad thing for other people. I've had good experiences with it and I've had bad experiences. When I was a kid going to school it wasn't drugs, it was beer. We used to go down and buy the big GI quart bottles and sneak down to the football field under the bleachers after dark and drink a quart of beer and get smashed and we thought that was the big thing because we weren't supposed to do it.

It's like sex. If you get all these don'ts and all of a sudden you do have a sexual experience and it happens to be a good one, then you start thinking, "Now why did they tell me 'don't' all the time?" It's exactly the same with drugs. They tell you, "Don't do them. They're dangerous, they're harmful, they're not good for you." Then some kid gets high on smoke and he has a beautiful thing and he says, "Well, gee, how come they're telling me all this? Maybe *every*thing they say is a lie."

We're not candid with our kids. We don't lay it on the line.

I don't know what *I'd* tell my own kids if I had them, though.

If we could hold it to an experimental type of thing it would be fine, but some kids. . . . There are kids that will experiment with anything and then just walk away from it and there are others that are just going to keep on with it. It has something to do with what's inside their heads. You're not going to stop kids from doing anything that they want to do.

There's a lot of idleness today with kids.

The main problem with drugs is not in the taking of them or in the using of them or even in the abusing of them. It's in the making of them — because they are illegal. Take heroin. You can go to the same dealer for five years in a row. The quality changes many times in those five years. One time it's cut so much. The next time it's cut *so* much. Another time, if he gets a shipment of pure heroin, it kills you. If he's a greedy person — and, remember, these men are in it to make money — he can buy a batch of rat poison and kill off a lot of people. You shoot it up and go off and die in the street and they just write if off as another dope addict.

The main thing most kids need is a friend. This thing we're trying to get going in Jamaica Plain — DEPTH — is a big love thing, a big-brother type of thing. Someone kids like to talk to. Someone kids respect. When such a person asks kids to do something, they'll do it, not because he's an authority but because the kids like him and look up to him. If I had a kid of my own I know I'd want to bring him up not by beating anything into him but by making him love me so much that he will do the right thing because he loves me.

There's a big thing today about love and brotherhood. People talk about it a lot but they generally don't really believe it. It's a farce. Look at your own circle of friends. I have a lot of friends. There's love there but not any great amount. Most people are into a self-love thing. You know, "Take care of yourself 'cause nobody else cares about you." That's why the brotherhood movement and the peace movement and all of those other things have drawn in the young people. They haven't yet realized that this is a materialistic world.

I've been riding bikes for over twenty years. Got to meet a lot of people. Most are only interested in getting ahead themselves. The big thing is to get married and have a family, go to school, and raise your kids. Well, I've been into that a couple of times in my life. Sorry to say it didn't work out. But most of my life was spent — not being a bum, I guess — but in just living. I've never been interested in money other than to have enough to live. If you live like that, you never have anything, really, but you get to know a lot about life and people. I have no regrets.

Mary Wilson — "You Don't Do Teen-agers Dirty." Mrs. Wilson is a very large lady. She has yellow hair, sometimes done in a ponytail. She is strong. Stormy. I remember when she was working at Playroom 81 how she flew into immaculate cleanups. She has phenomenal energy. An abundance of life. Laughs a lot. Everyone who knows her loves her because she is warm, honest, generous, and loyal. To a fault. The mayor's office, the welfare establishment, the housing authority, and a variety of psychiatrists and social workers find her excitable and irrational. I think that she cannot tolerate impersonality and isn't very good at playing games. She is the salt of the earth.

On psychiatrists:

"What kind of fool asks you what you cried about when you were three-years-old?"

Her own method:

I like young people. I love to be around teen-agers. When I lived over the Mission Project, these kids used to come over my house. God, they were the biggest crooks you'd ever want to see. Steal? Shit! I never said I wanted a television because if I said it, you *know* I'd 'a' had it. They'd go right into someone's apartment and take it out. I'm not lying.

They used to come in my house. I never let them drink because I feel this way: I wouldn't want someone to let *my* kids drink in their house. They used to come up and play records. They weren't bothering a goddamned soul. They'd tear up my house. But they were happy, right? Then when the cops started getting on my back and the housing authority started getting on my back and the mothers started getting on my back, it looked like I had to keep the teen-agers out for a while. Well, as soon as I did, every damned one of them got into more trouble than ever. But when I let them stay in my house they would never get in trouble.

Tommy* might say, "Shit, I'm going out to steal a car." And I'd say, "Tommy, don't go stealing no car. Please, come on, stay here and talk to me, will you? Tommy, you're drinking. You don't know that you're going to get hurt." He'd say, "Okay, I'll stay."

The kids used to tell me everything. Then the mothers used to call me a whore. "You're no goddamed good! Something's going on up there! Why are the teen-agers up there all the time?" I swear, there was never a goddamned thing went on in my house. Yeah, those kids used to steal. They used to steal everything but it never came in my house. I used to get blamed for it, though. Detectives were on my back. I was accused of everything. They said I had dope. They said I was letting them go to bed with each other. They said I was the biggest whore that ever lived in the damned Mission Hill project.

The kids still come over to my house now that I moved here to Bromley-Heath. First it was just a few kids. Then it got to be, oh, Jesus, twenty or thirty. I get confused with all the kids around. They'll all be over here tonight. They sit around; don't do nothing. They're all over twenty-one. They'll bring a couple of beers and talk crazy talk. One of the kids last week was taking acid. He was *way* out! I said to the boys, "Go get him. Bring him up here." I figured if we let him alone, he'd get in trouble. So he came up here and fell asleep. I don't let the kids take stuff like that. Not in my house they don't.

I was a wild teen-ager. I drank at sixteen. I did just what every kid on the street did. And I know what the cops did to us. Take us and punch our faces when we weren't even doing anything. Then they'd come up when we were playing cards and take our money off us. Or come up the hill and take our beer. I wouldn't trust cops as far as I could throw them. Kids just need a place to go where people leave them alone, without the cops hanging around.

You don't do teen-agers dirty. If you ever do them dirty they'll hurt you more than you could have ever hurt them. Kids never did me dirty. They would go out and steal anything from anybody. I'd leave forty, fifty dollars in my bureau drawer. You know, they never touch my money.

The mothers used to tell the kids: "Don't go near Mary." *Shit!* Then the kids got to be sneaks.

Judy (teen-ager):*   They'd rather see us out in the streets. Mary is like a sister to us. We know we can stay over her house. We can bring our boyfriends up here. She won't let them take pills or anything.

Mrs. Wilson: If I ever saw a couple in the bedroom with the door shut I'd have killed them. I used to take the broom out. The boys were scared of me!

Judy: We had a lot of good times. In the winter when it's freezing out, we could come up here and sit around and talk. We could tell Mary anything — even the boys could tell her.

Mrs. Wilson: A lot of these boys would tell me things — I never told a goddamed soul. Nothing. I used to get called down to that housing authority office about the kids robbing. But what am I gonna do? Go to court and say, "Yeah, he did it"? For what?

The manager at the housing authority used to say, "What do you do that the teen-agers are so attached to you?" I said, "Nothing. They sit up my house, drink Pepsi, talk a lot of bullshit, play the record player till they drive me out of my mind. You think I *like* having them there? Sometimes I could kick everyone of them in the ass. Sometimes I see them coming and I say, 'For crissakes, do you *ever* stay home?'"

Judy: Willie* took some pills one night. Mary started yelling at him and told him not to come around.

155

Mrs. Wilson: Some kids have been coming here since they
were fourteen. I moved. I MOVED! Wouldn't give
the bastards my address, my phone number, not a
goddamned thing. The bastards found me.

   If people would just leave these kids alone and
stop treating them like fools they'd be all right.
Trust. That's the biggest problem. The kids need
someone they can *trust* and not a lot of *bull*shit. I
remember what it was to starve to death, freeze to
death, and I really couldn't accept it. Then this one
psychiatrist told me that if I had a little hardship
growing up, I should accept it! What the *hell*?!

Aram Arsenian — Samaritan Storekeeper

Read *Archie* comics. There is a candy store where the kids hang
out. A place to buy a hamburger and a milk shake. The man
behind the counter is in his sixties, round, friendly, bumbling,
and in a fatherly sort of way is always trying to keep the kids
in line. Everybody loves him. He is decent, reliable, supportive.
He will give you credit when you need it. The shirt off his back.
Anything you need. He knows the kids take advantage of him.
But he loves and values each of them. A grandfather to the
neighborhood. Aram has given his life to children. "Hi, Pops."
An apron. Gray moustache. Sleeves rolled up.

   A homey little store. You can buy newspapers, used paper-
backs, some groceries. There's a jukebox, a cigarette machine,
some lawn furniture to sit on. A counter. Kids are on both
sides. Fixing an omelet for breakfast. Kids hanging around.
Hooking school. Aram tells them to go. Slight movement.
"Hiya, Doc. Wanna cuppa coffee?" Kids sitting around
listening to the jukebox. Aram horses around with one of
the Jones brothers. Pins his arms behind him. Both are
smiling. Aram says he's had enough and *never again!* A
warm atmosphere. Home.

   Whenever I'm in Jamaica Plain I like to stop in and see Aram.
Real life is very sentimental. Much more so than Hollywood

156

schmaltz would lead one to imagine. Also more heroic.

Aram's story:

I am an Armenian. I was born in Turkey. There was a massacre of Christian Armenians during the First World War. Kids were left on the desert to starve when their parents died hungry. The massacre was in the Jerusalem desert where you couldn't go back. You had to stay there because you were bottled up by the Turkish soldiers, Mohammedans, "Christians must die hungry." That was the slogan.

Out of twenty-three thousand, only three of us living today.

I was made an orphan. As time went along, I was adopted by the Arabs, the sheik, and I was forced to work for them. I made Lawrence of Arabia what he is today. I knew him well. I saw children on the desert starving. I picked them up one by one and sold them to Lawrence of Arabia for a dollar a head. He would give them to the American missionaries and the American Red Cross.

For over a year I stole from the rich. I hate to say it—it's an awful thing to say. When the sheik gave me the job to deliver bread to the workers, I used to steal sixty-six loaves each night. I hid sixty-six children in a cave behind the mountain. I used to give each one of them one loaf. Small loaves. That was all. That was a big thing for them to live on. I gave those kids one loaf. Out of the sixty-six, one, two died regardless.

It took me four years to get caught. I stole the bread for four years. From the rich. When I got caught, they whipped me. I still have a mark on my body. You must tell the truth or that's it. I told the truth. The judge was the one great Samaritan out of the whole rotten Mohammedan race. He put me on a horse and we went to the cave where the kids were living. The sheik came, too. I said to the kids: "I can't help you anymore. I'm caught."

The judge and the sheik spoke to the kids about the bread. "Yes," the kids said. "One loaf each day for each of us for four years." When the judge heard this, he grabbed the sheik. He said, "I want you to get all of these kids into some home. And this boy, Aram Arsenian, is not guilty. You have enough bread. You didn't miss what he took. He saved these kids. You should be honored that he worked for you. He worked for five years and you never paid him except for two meals a day. So he's entitled to those sixty-six loaves a day he stole from you."

From then on the sheik respected me as the highest one among his family. All his money went through me. That's how much he trusted me.

I've been here in Jamaica Plain twenty-three years. This was one of the roughest, toughest areas in the city of Boston. Even the banks when I asked for help would turn me down on account of the area. I run a general business. I was brought up the hard way and I know how to make money. I know the value of business. I don't expect to make a living on kids. They steal more than what I make from them. If I catch them, they pay. If they haven't got it, they haven't got it.

I'm not doing it for fun. I'm doing it because I know I'm helping some people somewhere along the line. I don't know where it will come out sooner or later but it will come out somewhere. When these boys go in the service, they know that someone has been with them all the time.

I correct their mistakes. I get them jobs. I help them with money. I don't expect to get it back. But you'd be surprised. As bad as people say they are, I get some money back. Maybe fifty percent. But kids are kids. I say to a kid: "You owe me money." It's a slogan. I can't remember how much they owe me. Sometimes they don't owe me. But it's up to them. If they say, "Okay, I owe you two dollars. I pay you tomorrow," tomorrow comes and they do pay back, once in a while.

These kids. I don't care who they are or what they are. They grow up. If we can wait. Wait until Uncle Sam calls them in the service. They come back brushed up, nice and clean. Different men altogether. Every one of them. They ask for references. And references I give them to every company. I get them jobs. They sometimes don't hold them too long. They steal, one way or another from the places I send them. But kids are kids.

When the boys go in the service and need money, they don't call their parents. Parents are poor. So they call me. Maybe three o'clock in the morning. Many times my wife and I have gone to the Western Union to send money wherever they are. Before they leave, I give them a ten-dollar bill, a carton of cigarettes, toothpaste, razor blades, shaving cream. And then I kneel down and pray for them to come back safe. And believe me, in twenty-three years I haven't lost one kid in any action anywhere in the world from out of this street corner. Must have been my prayer has done them good.

(Several times during the interview a rather husky, aproned teen-ager pops his head into the back room where we are talking and fires questions about prices of specific items. He is businesslike and appears to be fairly efficient.)

This boy, he broke in the store. He robbed me a thousand dollars. Damage was big. I didn't hold it against him but he got caught other places. That's the boy right there. I bail him out of the jail twice. The third time I said, "You go save yourself from now on because I done my duty to you. I save everybody once but you I did twice. Now, you help other kids to straighten up." He does his best. Many times when they're trying to break in the store nights he stands there. He'll say to them, "No one gonna touch here anymore. Even if I have to turn you guys into the law." Same kid which was a wrong kid. He don't get in trouble now.

I put signs in the store at nights. I know they're gonna break in. So I put a sign on all the machines and cash registers: "Take what you want. Don't break the machine. Come back again. Thank you.—Aram." The last time they broke in one of the crooks was here the next day having a coke.

159

I overheard him telling another kid: "Jesus Christ, there's no fun breaking in this store. Aram had this crazy sign on the machine: 'Take what you want. Don't break the machine. Come back again!' Aram took the joy out of robbing. I don't *like* those kind of signs!"

I like signs. I put a sign: "No profanity at any time. This means you! If you use, please go out thirty-one days yourself voluntarily, because if you don't I'll throw you out for a year! — Aram." But it didn't do any good. Kids take advantage. Don't think I don't slap them sometimes. Last week I slap one of them. I had to do it because he used profanity. He used it regularly. F—— this and f—— that. I couldn't take it anymore. I throw him out for thirty-one days and that hurts him. That just about kills him. He stands outside freezing. He won't do that anymore!

In a neighborhood like this, the best friends the kids have is not the law but, number one, the stores they associate with. The stores know their family, know them since the day they were born. If these stores have the patience, they'll accomplish a lot. But how many stores will do it? How many stores will step out of their way? How many stores will sacrifice their life? They won't. Maybe I'm one of the crazy fools.

I let the kids sometimes stay in my house. In my emergency room. Two, three days. I serve them. My wife says, "How long can you do this? All the time you bring me another one, another one, another one! When is going to be the end of it?" I said, "Thank God we could do something. I appreciate for your helping me out along the line." She has to put up with me because she loves me. Otherwise she would say, "This is it!"

Scotty McGlynn — "I Give a Damn"

I was at Lyman Reform School when I was seven years old. I've seen young kids being subjected to homosexuality. I've seen young kids being banged into the ground and kicked

160

and stomped on by the guards. From Lyman I went to Shirley and saw the same thing. I ran away from Shirley and stole a car and broke in someplace and was sent to an adult house of correction. That started my "nine house" bit, including a Bridgewater bit and a Concord Reformatory bit.

A kid grows up on the corner, has a bad homelife, and what does he do? He goes out and is top dog on the corner to get the love identification from others that he couldn't get at home. He makes his mark that way. He destroys the potential love and goodness that's within himself. It becomes just chaos.

A life of crime isn't very glamorous. I was scared to death. I was rebelling against a society that had thrown me to the dogs. Young kids from broken homes are put into an institution. They rebel against it because they feel that nobody gives a damn for them. This is what started me on my tour of crime.

At the age of twelve in the Lyman School I tattooed H*A*T*E on my knuckles because it was the only way that I could express what I felt. When a kid steals he's saying, "For God's sake, *help me. Love me!*" In the type of system we have now, there's not much being done to understand a kid. This society believes in punishment.

In the Lyman School, for every arithmetic problem we got wrong we used to get a whack on the hand with a big stick with tape around it as an incentive to learning. I had a completely rebellious attitude. I wasn't going to learn in that classroom. And I didn't. Eventually I ran away from the school.

The sexual tension is continuously present in prison and there is no escape from it. That's why when I first started doing time, I had to carry a pipe and a knife so I wouldn't get raped. But when I was there a few years, I was doing the same thing that the old-timers were doing. I dug kids. Most people are going to say, "Oh, man! Crazy fag son of a

161

bitch!" *Beautiful!* Let them say it. But I know what I am as a person. I know what I've been through. I know what society has put me through. Put a kid in an abnormal environment, make him grow up in that environment, and the worst in him will be brought out. I think it's normal to be a little bitter about it and it's good to express it because I need to get it off my chest. But instead of reacting blindly, and hurting myself and others, I have found a sufficient outlet in the Self-Development Group. I'm not scared to tell anybody how I feel.

(Scotty is a thin quick man. Twenty-eight. He looks you straight in the eye. Very intense. An occasional stammer, reflecting an urgent message that must be released with more power than speech machinery can handle. Hides nothing. Doesn't judge or ask to be judged. You are accepted totally, absolutely. His nerves have been tempered in a blast furnace. An angry man but you sense the profound humanity. The love.)

In 1963 at Concord Reformatory we were a group of guys doing time. Two men were doing big time for bank robberies. They sat down with each other once and just tried to relate honestly to each other. It made them feel like a million dollars after playing phony games all their lives. They discovered that if they made an effort to change their attitudes and their way of thinking they could be winners. They soon came to the conclusion that if two guys could relate honestly to each other, why couldn't ten do it? They brought in eight more guys, including myself, and this started the first Self-Development Group. We joined because we realized that if we didn't get off our lazy butts and do something for ourselves, nobody was going to come to our aid.

We called this group of ten guys "The Center Group." We have therapy meetings run entirely by cons. The chairmanship for the meeting rotates each week. We open with a moment of silence for the former Superintendent of Concord Reformatory. Then we say the preamble which

162

begins: "The Self-Development Group is composed of people voluntarily pledged to aid each other. . . ." We list the seven points that we try to live our lives by. One of these is picked as the topic for discussion at each meeting.

Now we have evolved a complete follow-up program on the outside in group therapy plus financial aid—a home if need be—and we assist a guy in getting a job. We stick to him. It's a lifetime membership. We're available anytime he needs us, night and day. Now we've reached out to other institutions and have similar programs going elsewhere.

The only way we've been able to evaluate our program is through the recidivism rate. From 1963 to the present the SDG (Self-Development Group) rate has been about 32.2 percent. The typical non-SDG rate is between 75 and 85 percent.

Who knows more about crime than an ex-criminal? We know what to do and we go out and do it. We don't have political ties like the state correctional institutions have. We're not scared to be put in the middle because we're a private agency. We sweated and struggled to put our group together and we don't want any professional takeover or any political takeover. We feel that we are closer to the problem than anybody because we have been through it. I *know* what a guy feels in his heart because I've been through sixteen years of hell.

Drugs deteriorated me. This is what I tell the kids. We don't try to hide the reality. If you do they won't get anything out of it. Mostly we try to shut our big yappers and listen to what the kid has to say. It is important only because *he* tells it. But he has to know that you're willing to take the time and the effort to listen and to try to understand him as a person, as a human being.

I would say that eighty percent of the programs for kids today stink. We tried to get our own program connected with the schools in South Boston. We went around to the classrooms relating our experiences. We even tried to get a program set up to help handle discipline problems, which we felt we could have done in a better way than school officials could. I have a feeling that they knew we could and that's one crazy reason why eventually they kept us from getting into the schools. Society puts up a big front: "Let's not let anybody know that we're having problems with our goody-goody kiddies!"

But when society damns someone they damn him forever. Calling a kid a delinquent crushes him into the ground with a sledgehammer. Society says: "Don't! *We* are in power! If you disobey, we will destroy you." That has been tried on us and we know very well that it doesn't work. It makes us *rebel* and *rebel* and *rebel!* It is a vicious circle. Instead, a kid must be told, "Look, man, I'm human, too. I make mistakes. Let met try and put myself where you are and see if I can be your friend and give you a little help."

We tried organizing kids of all ages in South Boston. We sat down with them. We let them know what they were doing to themselves and we listened to the many ideas that they came out with. Really *good* ideas. I've learned more about aspects of life from thirteen- and fourteen-year-old kids than I've learned from adults. That only happens when you put yourself down on their level and let them know: "Man, *I give a damn about you!*"

Arthur Eskew — Calvinist

I think the whole thing is based around your morals. I think the name of the game is being able to abstain from the things that are destructive to you. I think these are the kinds of things that make a man. He's supposed to be guided by logic. I think if he knows something is detrimental to him, I don't think he can teach it unless he can first apply the law to himself. I think a man working with a youngster must first police himself, and he must try to be as right as he possibly can be.

Religion is food, clothing, and shelter. In other words, religion is a way of life. The meaning of the word is to unite and do again those things that will cause you to survive. I believe the whole problem is a moral problem. This whole society produces the products it does because of the immorality that exists. Man's whole relationship to man is based on the fact that he's not moral enough to be a brother to man.

Religion is education. It's knowledge and understanding on how to sustain yourself in life rather than death. See, we have to unteach many of our youngsters that they must die in order to live. We tell the youngsters that they must maintain the kind of life they are fortunate to have and to try to nourish and take care of it because it is something that is very sacred.

Religion is making man get up out of his particular dead state and throw off the old colonialist role.

(Art Eskew is a Calvinist—a Muslim, I would guess—but what's the difference? It is important to him that the mind and body be disciplined. I have seen his program a number of times and get from it a sense of organization and purpose that is absent from most other programs. Emphasized is education, tutorial work. Dorzell Porter—"Chops"—a huge, friendly guy, works for Eskew and directs his boys' program. . . . Little boys ran almost in step around the gym under the leadership of one of them. Chops was upstairs talking with us. Later he came down and had them do exercises. When the boys were finished, they marched quickly to the pool tables. All sat down except two who efficiently removed the covers from the tables and put them away. Games ensued without squabbling. The boys were polite and friendly to visitors. . . . Chops is good at running the program because he has a natural magnetism. Kids adore him. But for Eskew, organization is ideological. It is to throw off shackles, build a nation, please God. Chops is not an ideologist. He believes simply in being "together.")

I tell you, I lean more toward the males because I know what it takes to build a nation. It takes *man.* He is the

165

leader. He is the born leader. He is the creative leader. Women have been conditioned to believe that no man, particularly a black man, has any kind of validation. They've been failed so much by what they've thought was men that anything that resembles this creature has no value at all.

I think that every man should arrive at the point where his life is not his own, where he's an integral part of something that has to go forward. He must be dedicated to our people, to a concern for the condition that they are in, and to getting them out of it. Everything that he has he must bring to this commitment in order to build a foundation. Such a foundation can be built in community centers such as this.

I really want to shout down the idea of developing the young black man's arms and legs. Let him sit down a bit. He's been running a lot. He's been dancing, too. I want him to sit down now. I want him to meditate and think. I want him to become aware of pain. Not the kind of pain where you take a Twinkie and cover your hunger. I would rather that he be hungry than get that Twinkie.

I don't know of very many educated black people. Most of them are *trained*. You can train a monkey but a *man* needs to be educated. This is why blacks do not know where their obligations are, because they're not educated. Education would automatically bring you back to where you're needed. Above all, if you have love and pride and dignity, education would automatically enable you to sustain yourself, your culture, enable you to reproduce. If you don't want to reproduce, you have no regard for yourself or for love or for anything. This seems to be the state that we are just coming out of. We have been dehumanized, deprived of education and therefore of culture and therefore of the ability to reproduce spiritually. And our young are still going through it. We'll lose two or three more generations.

What we have to do is cleanse ourselves of the things that make us greedy and then go out and seek the knowledge that will bring us scientific competence. I tell this to five- and six-year-old children. I tear down artificial greatness— the ability to destroy the earth many times. I question that and leave questions in the minds of the young. This is the main thing that our center is doing.

When I see a little one of ours that has not made it, the pain of that vision moves me to the point where I want to do something about it, and everything I have is then at that child's disposal. I know that my own survival rests in that little one. All of us together are one man, one people.

That feeling was not always with me. I was probably as vicious as any man in the streets at one time, trying to survive for myself. That meant, as Franz Fanon said, that I would strike out at the thing that reminded me most of my own horrible existence and that would be my own people. We can no longer do that.

The scientist is often thought of as being anti-God. In my way of thinking and teaching he is a person who is seeking God more vigorously than anyone else. He is seeking truth and this, in my opinion, is God. Science is where you find the truth and therefore where you find God. Black studies are beside the point—sugar coating on the real issue. Black studies departments are inviting our students into fields of endeavor that are after the fact, simply embellishments. Most black students are going into the liberal arts. Only very few are going into the sciences. Until they do this, however, we are never going to begin black capitalism.

God is important and should not be underestimated. I don't believe, for example, that two men can sit down and come to a reasonable agreement about how to govern themselves—a common law. I think that there has to be someone, some superior law, some superior being, that they both respect, high enough and with enough strength for chastisement for both men to fear and thus respect Him or it. I think that the only thing that governs man is fear. If he loses that fear he becomes an individual that is wrapped up in his own vanity.

You see, your life is not yours to dispense with as you wish. It does not belong to *you.* It belongs to the one who created it because he had a purpose for it. Viewed that way, you have less frustration and worry. You know what to expect and, because you study, you can understand why the white man is the way he is.

Curt Chapin— Natural Man

Yesterday, sprawled on the rug in the house at B.U. in which we hold our classes, one of the students, Denise, gave her report on Rousseau. I thought it was pretty good. I like Rousseau. Leo Stubbs—flamboyant, black, jazz musician, sensitive, flooded with images, ideas, plans—thought that Rousseau was full of crap. Unrelated to urban reality and hung up about women, Leo felt. Leo worked for Curt Chapin last summer at Camp Elbanobscot, in a program for urban-and-suburban boys. Leo thinks highly of Curt. Curt is Rousseau. I told Leo to think Chapin, not Rousseau. Leo rapped about how fantastic the guy is—how the first thing he does with kids when they get off the bus is run like crazy around the camp with them. Running, running, leaping, racing. Fast but everyone is together. Then the son of a bitch leads them all straight into the swamp. With all their clothes on. They just jump over a kind of little hill and there they are, chest deep in a bloody swamp. City kids. Well-manicured suburbanities. They follow Curt. Scared at first. Tentative. Slogging through the muck. Curt reaches out and grabs a frog. Bites its head off, skins it with his teeth, and then eats it raw just to show the kids that they can survive. Does the same thing with a snake. The kids are horrified but dig it. Curt is a magician. Thin, serious, late thirties. Full of wonder, enthusiasm, endless knowledge about things that are important. He knows archeology. You walk along with him and he drops to the ground, takes out his hunting knife, starts digging furiously in the dirt with it, and comes up with a chip from an Indian arrowhead or something.

He dropped out of a fine school system in something like the tenth grade and refuses ever to get legitimate credentials. He's waiting for an honorary doctorate from Harvard or Oxford or the Sorbonne. And he might get it, too.

Last year Curt and I worked together on a proposal for a school. It was really all Curt. I just got him to do it. He hates to write so we tape-recorded, edited, added here and there, and it was finished. Curt's utopia. Jan Staiano, from the Elbanobscot Foundation, worked with us, too. The idea was that the Foundation would sponsor the school, give their land, and we would find funds elsewhere. But the whole thing hinged on Curt and, sadly, he became interested in other things. Like his Eskimo exchange program, for example. He wants to send Brookline kids (he is a special-class teacher in Brookline) to Frobisher Bay to learn seal hunting. Frobisher Bay kids would come to Brookline and learn whatever it is that Brookline kids learn. Maybe during the summer his camp would have an Eskimo kayaking counselor. He spent a month in Frobisher Bay at the end of last summer, returned with endless enthusiasm and knowledge. I can easily understand why a man like that could not be tied down to a school. But no one else could do it. Curt's ideas are unique and they can only be carried out by Curt. Asking anything else of him is like asking Bach to come up with ideas for concertos for other people to write. Curt is like Bach.

* * *

The meat and bones of Curt's school idea:

The site for the proposed program is Camp Elbanobscot.

The camp is situated in Sudbury, Massachusetts, roughly forty minutes—twenty-five miles—from downtown Boston. It consists of one hundred acres of mixed woodland, meadow, marsh, and deciduous forest and forms a peninsula on the Sudbury River. All sorts of animal and plant life abound in the area. The three hundred acres immediately behind the camp are owned and controlled by conservation groups and the Commonwealth of Massachusetts, and are available for program use. The Sudbury River and adjacent wetlands are part of the Great Meadows National Wild Life Refuge and consist of approximately two thousand acres.

Participants would be boys, black and white, city and suburban, ages ten and eleven. Criteria for selection would include current inadequate school performance and judged ability for much higher level academic and/or leadership functioning.

Examples of the sorts of activities that might take place:

— Designing and making tribal garments out of scrap leather, old furcoats, etc.
— Developing group rituals and traditions, ceremonies and folklore. Bull sessions in which mutual problems can be discussed and resolved honestly, openly and with as much intensity as one may wish to generate.
— Evolving a camp bartering, trade, or monetary system.
— Archeological and nature study of the camp area on foot, canoe, or snowshoe (whichever is appropriate).
— Eating meals with one's hands from a community pot.
— Killing trash fish with clubs in the manner of pre-agrarian man.

— Swimming in the nude.
— Building boats out of twigs and brush and taking trips in them.
— Learning how to survive for periods of time in the the woods in various seasons without modern implements.

In general, the emphasis will be on adventurous activities which are strongly masculine in tone and develop a highly cohesive, rugged, swashbuckling group in a setting which is as unlike school in every visible respect as possible. The camp activities will each carry with them a high degree of ecstatic emotion and will be designed to enhance "Huck Finn" fantasies. All children no doubt have participated vicariously in such adventures but to be actually *there* is to enjoy freedom and pleasure to the extreme.

(My son Michael went to Elbanobscot last summer and loved the swamp walk and adores and worships Curt but was saddened that much of the camp was "just like school. First we had assembly, then we went to arts and crafts and then we played baseball and then we went swimming." Michael hates schedules and time limits. I brought this up to Curt, sternly critical. How could you do this to my son? Curt explained that during the summer he's no longer his own man. Got to administrate a big frigging program. Felt he was more creative when he was merely a poor nature counselor. Rousseau caged. Oh, the horror of it! But the *school* will be different. An antidote to the foul plagues of bureaucracy, capitalism, or whatever.)

Evolution of the Group:

A.   Primitive Banding

The boys will come to the school as individuals with no prior knowledge of the other members and only the foggiest notion of the nature of the program. The first goal will be to help the children relax and, in the presence of each other, to regress to whatever primitive stage of social

171

organization is appropriate to their needs. Spurred by
anxiety and uncertainty, much running around and silliness
will no doubt occur. With direction from the teacher,
however, potential chaos and fragmentation will be transmut-
ed into orgiastic group activities such as bonfire building.
Individual anxiety becomes group spectacle involving
ritual cataclysm as if to stay the impact of bad magic.
Real relationship among the boys is virtually nonexistent at
this stage but being with others provides some safety and
considerable, though undifferentiated, pleasure.

B.   Pre-Tribal Level

Gradually the rudimentary rituals will evolve into something involving a degree of give and take and some real
relating. Children will eat out of a common pot with their
hands. They will hunt together for foods—grasshoppers, frogs,
etc.—and learn to cook them. They will have to paddle
together to get to the other side of the river to find favorable
campground.

Increasingly they will find themselves in situations
requiring cooperation. Increasingly, too, the nature of the
cooperation will become more complex so that what begins
as need for protection and immediate pleasure becomes
interactive and involved with building for future gratification.
Through interdependent work, tasks are accomplished that
lead to better things for the individual and the groups than
previously thought possible.

C.   Tribal Level

The trend of development after arrival at the pre-tribal
stage is not merely toward increasing complexity and
richness but toward the evolution of rules which guide
behavior rather than the temporary transactional arrange-
ments that characterized the pre-tribal period. Further,
learning is accelerated and aided by developing habits of
ordering, categorizing, and recording to preserve for history,
a sense of which has begun to emerge.

Traditions are manufactured almost daily. Children nominate certain stones "lucky," name their best fishing grounds and preserve valuables in a secret cache in a hollow tree which is also named.

As the tribe develops, certain crafts emerge. The children have to produce a lot of the things which they use. Certain individuals may become recognized for their skill in starting fires while others are known for their proficiency in using leather. A bartering system arises as the maker of wooden spears trades his product for that of the fisherman.

By now the group has become highly interactive and the needs of each individual have to some extent been submerged in accordance with the purposes both of the larger group and of other individuals. Compromise and arbitration sessions occur. A tribal system of law evolves for the regulation of behavior and the resolution of conflict. Interestingly, the system arrived at may or may not have its correspondence in American culture. Ownership disputes may be settled by a judge in accordance with law and facts, or on the other hand by a spear-throwing contest contingent on strength and accuracy!

D.   Civilization and Enlightenment

As time goes on the culture becomes increasingly utopian. Subsistence gives way to learning and the arts. Relationships are built up among the group leaders, the children, and between the camp and the outside community through numerous trips and studies. The trappings, the rituals, the clothes, the belief system, and the morale are retained but more sophisticated and more cosmopolitan material is introduced. Learning may be increasingly formal but spurred by an élan which is derived from the developed group and in accordance with the needs and interests of the individual learner.

By now the children have developed considerable competence, their egos are strengthened and their confidence is enhanced. They have mastered many new skills. They have formed new and enjoyable relationships and have come to terms with physical and psychological reality of an extreme and immediate sort—*they have met death*—and have emerged joyfully. Inquisitiveness and learning have come directly from interaction with the world and the sensations of one's own experiences. Learning has begun at its most elemental level the necessity for survival. Finally, a peer group has been formed which actually supports learning, a relatively rare phenomenon in American culture.

Mildred Lau — Teacher

(The learning center operates as part of the Bromley-Heath Neighborhood House under the direction of Mr. Arthur Eskew, mentioned earlier. Mildred Lau was a master's level student at Boston University in the Special Education Department, and along with her colleagues, Wendy Siebert and Ernest McNeil, developed the center, an informal supplementary school, as part of her master's degree program.)

After general assembly, I took my kids to the library. They quickly set themselves to work on the Halloween play. It is about a war between witches and a mad doctor and his monsters. After we talked as a group and vaguely established the where, when, and who of the play, the four witches went to a table while the mad doctor and his four monsters went to another table, each side to write its own plot.

Diane,* the head witch, was wonderful and managed to get all the little witchy minds to work.

The monsters were very excited and started to throw off a million great ideas:

"We're going to put on this play and we'll have a big party!"

"We'll make up invitation cards for parents and print up programs with pictures!"

"What about costumes?"

"What about lighting the room?"

"Wow! We've got to sweep this place up!"

"We can sell refreshments!"

Minds were alert. Ideas flooded in. I had to remind them that before we could do anything we had to create the play. It somehow didn't register.

"Listen, kids, we've got to figure out what happens in the play!"

"Well, the witches and the monsters each try to get the kids' candy!"

"And what do they do with the candies?"

"They poison them and everybody dies!"

"Naw, I think everybody should make friends!"

When I asked Sally* what she wanted to be in the play, she said, "Ghost." But under the influence of the other kids, she became a monster instead.

For the first part of the afternoon, she busied herself on a piece of paper. She didn't just pick up a pencil and draw or write as one is supposed to do. She took one, tried it out, threw it away, tried another one, and so on until she went through every one of them. A ritual.

Then slowly, elaborately she printed "Sue" on the corner of the page. Underneath she drew a picture of Sue. She continued writing other titles and drawing pictures under them.

She comes over to show me what she has done. But she doesn't come brashly. Nobody can see her paper. She hides it coyly; protects it from view. She shows it secretively, furtively.

She has so little self-confidence! She is in conflict between thinking that she has done a good job and wishing that she *could* do a good job. When I said, "Sally, this is beautiful! You are really good!" she replied immediately with an abrupt, uncompromising, "No, I'm not!"

175

It is painful for me to realize how little self-confidence she has and how low her expectation is that the world will respond to her in a positive way. I cannot help but be appalled by the realization that we are dealing with an enormously delicate psychological being. I try to think of her in the classroom situation. How can she possibly survive unscarred? How callous the class routine! We expect her to sit quietly while the world manhandles her sensitive tissues and open sores. Will she ever get an opportunity to experience the gratification of a well-accomplished job that is her own?

After her names and drawings she took another piece of paper and laboriously wrote: "This is a fat man." She was so excited that she wrote a whole sentence by herself without a mistake. She decided to repeat the feat and copied the sentence again. She spent a lot of time smiling and gazing at her writing. This was a new experience for her, I imagine. She was totally absorbed, tongue sticking out. She could not be distracted. In fact the rest of the group was pretty noisy and rambunctious.

This is so different from the earlier scenes of total and impotent frustration when the child makes a mistake or simply does not like what he's done—the angry crumbling of the paper into a ball and flinging it to the floor. The act of utter rejection of one's product, of one's self. The inability to be satisfied with a step in the right direction. The all-or-none principle. It is not enough to erase a mistake and try again. You have to destroy it physically, concretely, erase with a passion, tear the paper into shreds. Unless destroyed, the permanence of a rejected drawing, of a rejected self, is too threatening.

Nancy,* an older girl, is pretty good at drawing. A number of the younger kids waited in line for Nancy to draw a witch on their paper. What counted was a nicely drawn witch and not the intrinsic joy of creating your own witch, whatever it may look like. What counts is not the process, not the feelings and the pride in self. The kids have the system well internalized.

In the back room a group of six kids were playing with a spelling game I brought in. It was a complex game and inappropriate for these kids. But they didn't mind. I handed them the box; they figured out that it was a spelling game and they took over.

Johnny* took the shaking container and shook the lettered dice up in it. Another kid took the sand timer and set it appropriately. Johnny started making a word. I suggested that somebody write down the words. The suggestion was quickly implemented. Johnny was madly making words and others helped eagerly. They got very excited when they completed a word. They were not in the least hung up about spelling correctly. Not once did anyone ask me or any other adult whether a word was spelled correctly or not or, indeed, if it really existed.

Once in a while, somebody would raise a doubt: "Are you sure it's 'fot'?" Another kid would answer indignantly: "Of *course*, it's 'fot,' dope; 'fot' is like when you beat a kid up!" I didn't see any reason why they shouldn't spell "fought" as they pleased and, since enthusiasm for learning was at such a high pitch, I was content to leave well enough alone.

They played nicely, took turns, and played for about two hours, excited all the time. Most of the words were two and three letters long; a very few were over five letters. When the timer ran out, they counted the number of words written down during the three-minute period and someone else took a turn. When there was a hassle the group decided whose turn it should be and the kids concerned would accept the verdict with minimal resistance.

I was able to leave the room frequently and for prolonged periods.

I later saw their lists of words. Only a few of them were

misspelled and even fewer were nonexistent. Mistakes
generally were logical, understandable ones. They used the
same words for several games and stuck pretty much to easy
ones, but it was nevertheless a significant and valuable
event.

It was first of all a rare experience in pleasant and coopera-
tive school behavior. There was a common goal that was
created by the whole group and no one else. All members
participated and thrived on their own consent and
motivation.

They experienced the pleasure of being in total control
over the situation. Not only did they themselves create the
rules of the game but they created rules for the words themselves, for the spelling. For a change the words were under
their power and not the other way around. They didn't
have to confront any words they were afraid of. They
created them and they were in control. There was a feeling
of mastery and, for a few hours, independence from the
rest of the world.

It was a strange day in that the kids were so busy by
themselves that the other workers and I almost felt out of
place. It was a fantastic feeling! I caught myself tiptoeing
around, afraid to break the magic spell. When they came to
show us their masterpieces, I got nervous. I didn't want to
impose my judgement and disrupt the blissful pattern of
independence.

The children are much better judges than we are of
their own abilities, strengths, and weaknesses. When they
are ready to take up challenges, they do so even if they
also demand our support and encouragement.

Chapter Six

RUMINATIONS AND OBSESSIONS

Clarification and Evaluation

The book is sometimes written in an ironic style but there *is* a serious statement here somewhere. Let's see if we can find it.

How about:

"We are not doing what we say we want to because our operations are not related to our stated goals; hence neither are our outcomes."

A straight, clear statement and certainly honest . . . (but of course the main thing is the mood, the sense of unrelatedness and the spinning of wheels).

(There is so much that needs to be said and so little time.)

(I wish that time did not have to be the adversary.)

* * *

There was a boy in Newton five or six years ago. I was a school psychologist and he was a juvenile delinquent. One day he announced: "Doc, I could be a better psychologist than you!"

"How so?" I asked.

He said, "Well, you go around in those horn-rimmed glasses, those tweedy suits, and you use those big college words. I mean, you're trying; you're a nice fellow. But you can't speak the language. And the kids don't dig you like they dig me. I can help them because I'm from the same neighborhood and I lived the same life and I know them. You see what I mean, Doc?"

"Yes," I agreed, "I do see. You are probably right."

"Doc," he continued, "I've thought about it and I've decided that I would like to be a psychologist or a psychiatrist or a social worker; in a word: a Shrink!"

"But," I protested bureaucratically, "you must realize that at the moment you are on the perpetual verge of disaster in high school and, although obviously talented, you will probably not graduate. To be a shrink you must not merely finish high school but you must go on to college for four years and you must even continue well beyond college into something called graduate school for another two to five years. In other words, if you wish to be a shrink, you have at least another seven years of schooling ahead of you."

"Jesus," he murmured. "Why all that?"

"Well," I explained, "you must be certified by the profession and you must be licensed by the state and. . . ."

"Shit, man," he shot back. "You mean you gotta get a fucking license to be fucking nice to people!?"

* * *

Prospectus for a Proposal
"Nodes of Possibility"
I. Problems with Many Current Programs
   A. They are invented with little concern for the life-style of the community which is often dissonant with the implicit life-style of the program's authors.
   B. They are either too small, experimental, insignificant, or too large, bureaucratic, hence oblivious to the client.
   C. They do not grow organically in accordance with the developing needs and consciousness of the client

population. They originate instead full-blown in accordance with the needs of a remote second party such as a government agency, a foundation, a school system, or a university.

D. They do not provide the means for self-sustenance either in terms of funding, ideology, or personnel. Outside resources must constantly be poured in. Typically, little of value remains.

E. Although local agencies are often "involved," it is only the official ones. Informal associations such as bridge clubs and street-corner societies are seldom included. Yet in many neighborhoods informal associations of these sorts may be far more significant in the daily life of the people.

F. They are run either by professionals or by "new career" emulators of professionals. The fecund homeliness of the family is all too often missing.

G. Professionals, those having needed skills and resources, are only rarely utilized effectively. Instead of imparting useful knowledge on request, they become irrelevant but bossy missionaries.

H. Labels are often taken much too seriously. The client becomes arbitrarily fragmented. (E.g. It must be decided whether the client is an addict, a school dropout, unemployed, or emotionally ill . . . and if so what kind.) Services are rarely provided according to emerging need patterns, globally, flexibly, and informally. . . .

IV. Summary

A rather unspecific but potentially comprehensive youth program has been proposed. It is less a program, in fact, than a framework within which programs might develop in accordance with local style and requirements. The framework has three essential components:

A. Drop-in centers. Places where youth can "be themselves" and which can evolve in various ways —

toward learning, therapy, employment, recreation, or all of these or more. The center is a "node of possibility."

B.   Problem-solving discussion groups (Resolve A Problem or RAP sessions), which in turn can evolve into drop-in centers or other forms, all of which in turn will evolve. The RAP groups serve as forums for ideas as well as communications exchange centers. The RAP groups are also "nodes of possibilities."

C.   The summer place. A remote cauldron of creativity, encounter, and silence where new perspectives can be gained.

The principles which guide these programs are self-help, respect for local conditions, and a faith in the effects of supportive human interaction.

Funding would be centrally coordinated, community controlled, flexible, and only marginally adequate until a given program could show signs of viability and significance. Then funding would be provided more generously at the same time as monetary sources would be developed within each program.

(You shittin' me, man?)

* * *

It was the informality that was most important. The fact that each morning five or ten ladies and a few guys would come together for a meeting. The meetings would always have a formal structure but we could never make it work that way. People seemed to enjoy the opportunity to chat over coffee. There are formal organizations and there are informal organizations. There are organizations that dominate and suppress and there are organizations that are as to people as conversation is to a campfire or to cigarette smoke or to modern jazz.

* * *

182

It is expected that an institution designed closely enough to the specs of the client population will serve the function of drawing people together. If the demands of the structure are possible and inviting, people, looking outside of themselves to tasks, brushing up against others, sometimes conflicting, sometimes collaborating, will gradually adjust, function more and more expertly with regard to tasks and more and more gracefully with regard to one another. Task competence — or movement toward it — will lead to interpersonal competence if tasks require people to work together.

Thus particular words are not important. The general thrust over time *is*. Even more important is the question: "Does the structure invite the kinds of behaviors that are wanted?" *What* is wanted? No one wants chronic squabbling. No one wants to feel that options are closed. The feeling that "there's nothing to do" is devastating and unpleasant.

So the real goal is an interpersonal one — similar to what many conventional therapists state: to free people to function on higher levels in terms of their own continually evolving needs; at the same time to feel that they are living purposefully, actualizing themselves, being part of others and allowing others to be part of them. A goal statement such as this can unravel endlessly. Perhaps Freud's "To love and to work" is the best encapsulation of all that. People vary, but no doubt purpose born of affection and productivity is a pretty basic, universal need.

The institutions that we are concerned about in this book are not the large ones. These are pretty difficult to come to terms with, inevitably concerned with their own perpetuation, lost in corridors of bureaus, fouled in tangled fishnets of relationships; they simply cannot spill over into enhancement, except as an accidental by-product. The boss, threatened and threatening, feared and fearful, envied and jealous, "an old, mad, blind, despised and dying king."

We are concerned instead with little institutions: primary

groups. Schools, as Emile Durkheim points out in seeming contradiction, serve an important socializing function precisely because they require that children perform in accordance with impersonal social rules. Families can only *partially* prepare children to function in a complex culture. Why then the present emphasis on primary groups?

The nuclear family is simply not doing very well. Stresses on it are overwhelming, perhaps the most formidable of which is the family's very smallness and, paradoxically, apart from the need of children to have nurturant parents, there is little interdependence. Parents seem to have no *need* for children or for each other. A thin gruel of psychological sustenance is obtained through a myriad of temporary, shallow, and interchangeable relationships: the people we work with, go to school with, travel in the car pool with, meet at lunch, have cocktails with, live next door to, go to bed with. But we are not close to anyone long enough to develop an instinctive sense of another or bonds of group camaradeship. Intimacy is designed exclusively for family life, but the unit is too small and the attractions of the larger world too great. We feel that we must experience as much as possible, frantically to advertise the trappings of human success. Having only one — woman, child, family, person — is incompetent PR, suggesting soul poverty, loneliness. We must continually search elsewhere but we continue to find only soul poverty and loneliness.

A better thrust is perhaps toward the construction of minute institutions, designed to supplement, strengthen, and perhaps even to substitute for the nuclear family. Larger institutions such as school and industry are to be ignored and left to socialize people for the big world in their customary way. But in the interstices between the individual and the skyscraper we propose to find room for a matrix. Harvey Pressman calls for subversive "surround schools," as in Jewish and Chinese communities.

184

Our concern, then, is not with what is *said* to whom, but as in theater or architecture, we are concerned with where individuals *stand* in relation to each other. It is a spatial design problem. Tentatively we propose to create *on purpose* small spontaneous groups which would *do* something to change the world, not contemplate, confront, or experience. In the course of doing *real work* collaboratively, it is predicted that people will interact, differentiate roles, and feel a sense of belonging.

It is further suggested that a splendid possible task for such groups may be child care! Care of others, but in the course of caring, each caretaker is also cared for by the very fact of the presence of others. In other words, a climate of care is to be created in which distinctions between cared for and caring are gradually erased, as in a good family. However, leadership is maintained by the elders so that the group can be perpetuated, traditions can be handed down, and young people can have models and expectations to grow into.

We have mentioned a few groups that seem to be at least partial examples of what we are proposing: The Playroom, Nick's, Dick's, Art Eskew's. What is most important in such groups is the feel, the atmosphere, and that which is tangential, elliptical, and over time. Groups need to be cured, like stinky cheese or good ham, so that eventually they are delicious. Ups and down have rather less significance than what they are growing into and what side effects they are having on participants and community morale. Even though a given group may fail, go completely under, one or two individual members may have been drawn sufficiently out of their cocoons to make more probable their vigorous participation in a new emerging group. Hence the original effort, by its effects on *them*, may in this sense be successful.

Finally, from the public health point of view the most strategic "population at risk" is the adolescent. In biologic and social crisis, they provide us with a chance to reach the parents of the next generation before they have children. By training teen-agers, in need of useful work, to deal competently with children, we are, in effect, training a cadre of parents to become first-rate before they have anything invested in their errors. Further, teen-agers who have grown up in ordinary neighborhoods and have gone to ordinary schools stand as a precise fulcrum between the generation of their parents and the generation of their children. That is, they are close enough to the world they grew up in to understand it intimately. At the same time, looking into the future toward responsibility for others, they are motivated to improve upon what they knew. Their plan for renewal, because based in the reality of cultural style, is likely to make considerable sense.

A focus on youth, I would think, is just right for the community mental health architect.

* * *

There is a child in a second grade-classroom, an average suburban classroom. He has an IQ of 110. He has blond hair, brushed straight down toward his eyes. He has lots of freckles, especially around his nose. He wears chinos and a striped polo shirt and white sneakers. He is seven years old, or will be next month. He has a few friends but not close ones. When they get together they seem to run around a lot, tussle and giggle. His name is Billy.*

Billy's teacher is concerned with him because he is having considerable difficulty with arithmetic, spelling, and reading. In other words, he's an average American kid, screwing up in school.

Billy's parents are nice enough. Mother sits at home, watches her two younger kids, cleans house, gossips with the neighbors, wishes she had finished her master's degree in

186

English so maybe she could get a part-time job as a librarian. The sink is stopped up. She's in the kitchen, chin on her folded arms, watching the plumber who is strong, masterful, graying, fiftyish. She's musing. . . .

Billy's father is in the restaurant supply business. He's a junior partner in a small firm started by his granduncle. He rightly feels that he knows the business better than the old man but is given no opportunity to show his competence, to assume leadership. His granduncle is threatened by ambitious younger men and so has effectively isolated Billy's father. The business will ultimately be passed on to a conservative, pasty-faced fellow, whose dyed black hair is combed with foppish precision from the part straight across the top of the head so that it almost camouflages a large bald area.

When Billy's father comes home at night he feels tired, frustrated, and vaguely agitated. He needles his wife about chili con carne for supper again. He's never liked chili con carne.

Billy has nothing to do after school. He wanders around with some of his friends, mostly younger children, maybe bums a dime from Mom and goes to the drugstore for an ice cream cone. Sometimes goes to another kid's house but there's not much happening there, except television for a while. Comes home and hits his four-year-old sister because she's playing with his toy monster-maker machine and she *knows* he doesn't want *any*body touching his stuff. Mother has *had* it with Billy hitting his sister! Always picking on her. Mom screams. Billy hits his sister again. Mom grabs Billy. Spanks him. Billy flails; tries to hit Mom. She spanks him again. Billy cries. Screams. Runs up to his room. Slams the door. Throws some blocks against the wall, narrowly missing the window. Mom sits, puts her head in her hands and sobs; fingers dug in scalp, hair down to elbows, swaying gently, irregularly.

Billy's mother and father were called in by the teacher and told that unless Billy picked up he would have to repeat

187

second grade. She was concerned about his immaturity. Suggested the child guidance clinic in town. "They might be able to offer some professional help."

The clinic has a cold, Sears Roebuck Victorian waiting room. A grandfather's clock, light-green walls, and a dignified portrait of "The Founder". You would never know that they deal with children. Shrinks appear in brown sports jackets and dark pants, white shirts and striped ties. Smiling delicately, they slip away with their patients, each to his own sensibly arranged office — a desk, a telephone, and some nice toys. If only they painted the waiting room yellow, red, purple, orange, and polka-dot blue. And if it were little and warm, like a snug, protective cave; a harbor from the storm.

The people at the clinic rightly view Billy's problem as connected with his parents' marital stresses. Play therapy is suggested for Billy and family counseling for his parents. The social worker even offers to consult occasionally with Billy's teacher. A good plan for good people.

Tension at home reduces. Billy's school work eventually a bit.

But next year things take a turn for the worse.

Then they somehow improve by themselves.

Then they get worse again.

Billy is ten.

Mother is bored.

Father is tired, looks drawn; his face is lined, sagging.

They have few friends.

Stuck to each other. Shackled.

Mother dreams of boyfriends she had in college, nags interminably; cries a lot at night when the family is asleep.

Father goes to Chicago for business . . . often. With his secretary.

It doesn't help.

Things drag.

* * *

188

My God! If *these* people aren't being helped, who is? What about those who live in filth and utter degradation?

* * *

What if we gave Billy a place to play in the afternoon? Something to do. Lots of interesting people around. A lively atmosphere. All sorts of adults, young and old ones who drink coffee and chat and seem to enjoy each other's company and talk with the kids and read to them and work with them.

What if Billy's mother had someone or lots of people to talk with during the day and to share her child-rearing duties with?

If the awful sense of isolation left them. . . .

If there were a sense of other people. . . .

Maybe purposes would become clearer. . . .

Even father's work might make sense. . . .

And Billy might do better. . . . Who the hell knows?

There need to be small groups of people who *like* each other and talk, function together. Enjoy each other's company. Have fun. Particularly after a hard job well done. Together. Spirit of the commune. The kibbutz. The Gorki Colony. Of *course,* there are dangers. It is difficult to define roles when people, used to being lonely, are drawn so close. How do you keep it from being oppressive?

Perhaps if we start with people, a basement, and a vague idea. . . .

* * *

Biases re: Community Mental Health
I.   Ambivalence About Institutions

   On the one hand it is important to be inconspicuous but identified with the community, "as a fish to water" but on the other hand it is necessary to maintain a degree of

189

remoteness and old fashioned professionalism. Partly it is a question of ineradicable class differences between the mental health worker and his client community and partly it's a question of effective tactics. From a slightly "above the battle" stance one remains a bit less myopic — on some issues — than those blinded by the cannon smoke, and hence a better advisor when honesty is sought. Besides, despite a considerable degree of accept- ance — and maybe even because of it — people will *not* let the professional drop his title. He remains "Doc" or "Teach" no matter how much he insists on a first name relationship. It is a distancing maneuver, as well as a recognition of the reality of distance. At the same time it may be an expression of honest respect, or even affec- tion. Uncomfortable though it may make the radical pro- fessional, people seem to need to structure aristocracies.

II. Who Is Professional in What?

Shall we define a professional simply as one who does well what he says he can do, who can pause to reflect and consciously to evaluate, and finally, who is paid for his services by a client or patron? This distinguishes him on the one hand from the "expert," who is merely competent, and on the other hand from the "entre- preneur," who is merely paid. Another but related issue is that of credentialing. The public wishes to know prior to the purchase of services if the seller is capable of performing as advertised. The soundest guarantee is, of course, previous performance, but since this is difficult to assess in such complex, private arts as counseling and psychotherapy, we have developed a quite invalid system dependent not on *task* competence but on *academic* performance. There is no demonstrable relationship between the two. One might indeed argue that in some fields an inverse relationship exists — that is, the greater the academic skill the less probable it

190

might be that a given individual will perform adequately as, say, a community mental health worker. Such an hypothesis is at least entertainable if not entertaining.

III. What Are Some Tasks of a Community Mental Health Professional?

   a) Gadfly — the Community Mental Health Professional hides in the crevices, takes readings, and whispers advice to others. He is a stimulator, a catalyst, an *agent provocateur.*

   b) Social Scientist — he is not a therapist although he may occasionally help someone through a crisis or make a referral. His focus is on the community as a *whole* and the ebb and flow of contending forces which both enhance and detract from that community's viability.

   c) Guerrilla General — his thinking is applied, ruthless, and economical; devious but unassailably honest. He thinks strategically. . . .

IV. Tolerance of Ambiguity and Absurdity
   Despite overt strivings for change and revolutionary words, things have a way of remaining remarkably the same. Intergenerational conflict is resolved when the kids become parents.

* * *

Nick says that it is inaccurate to think of bikies as Nazis. They are pirates.

> A fig for those by law protected
> Liberty's a glorious feast
> Courts for courts were erected
> Churches built to please the priest!

> Robert Burns, *The Jolly Beggars*

I only believe in piracy with a small part of me. It is difficult to reconcile swashbuckling rape, pillage, and murder with the altruism referred to earlier, which tends to imply a respect for the rights of others. Further, despite *A High Wind in Jamaica,* it is difficult seriously to view Bluebeards and Captain Hooks as the best of all child care workers. They have advantages but some probable drawbacks as well. I would imagine, for example, that pirates would not show the consistency and dogged responsibility of trained career teachers.

The most refreshing thing about outlaw bands is their absolute refusal to attribute legitimacy to those institutions so many of us find irritating. Many of us wish we could be so absolute in our evaluations.

Many of us try to emulate them But it takes something. You have to be either so goddam poor that you have "nothing to lose but your chains." Or you have to have another job tucked away somewhere. Or you just take off with the fucking raggle-taggle gypsies, oh, knowing deep down inside that since you have been properly brought up you can always return. Armed with suburban optimism, you can descend to any depth or rise to any height. You always feel snuggly-safe.

The real poor don't fool around. If you got a decent job, baby, hold on to it and shut up. A black friend advised from self-knowledge: never be dependent on feedback from the boss or from peers. A lonely existence. It means pressing down immense quantities of fine, blue, irrepressible anger. Anger on a fat stomach, however, is a luxury; a gourmet's delight. I come home properly catharted. If busted, I will show the surprise and outrage of the rich.

* * *

My wife raised an important question about "brotherhoods." Mary points out that such organizations are exclusionary.

Those who belong are "brothers" but those who don't are thereby dehumanized and can properly be kicked, spat upon, and even murdered. In defining the good guys and the bad in such absolute terms one is opening the door to a vast increase in chauvinism and brutality. These are perhaps dangers to be weighed against mutual understanding, support, euphoria, and political power. Similar problems are present in the trade-union movement, Zionism, Black Power, and women's rights groups. But doesn't love for humanity have to begin with love for self, then for family, peer group, and the larger culture? Perhaps some form of practice in respect for the rights of others within a visible in-group must precede allegiance to mankind. Worrisome, however, is the mystique which proclaims superiority for the particular in-group, and its ability — if not its eagerness — to *destroy* all outsiders. All outsiders are considered threats.

Last night at a dinner party we met a history professor who was a student in Germany in the early days of the Nazi ascendancy. The romantic appeal of the Nazis was described again as I had heard it described before. The uniforms, the jackboots, the idealism, the invincibility. I told him of the motorcycle clubs and he was easily able to see the parallel. However, he wondered if perhaps man, originally a hunter, was not simply acting in accord with his racial unconscious.

"Do such groups *necessarily* become malevolent?" I wondered. He wasn't sure but doubted it. "Saint Francis D'Assisi was a hippie," he said.

* * *

Art Eskew believes in building a black community through internal discipline. Others believe in self-realization. How is one to evaluate? What makes sense? Perhaps the answer has to do with particular people. Some need some things. Some need other things.

Take the bikies, for example. The other day we had a session of our Harvard Extension-sponsored seminar for community youth workers. Three bikies came down, two from one club, one from another. The two men from Club A told us tales about drug importation, harassment of and by the police, free love, and things like that. "We are the Jesse Jameses and the Wild Bill Hickoks of this age," they told us. "When you talk to us, man, you're talking to organized crime. We don't want to do *any*thing constructive." They added, "We only showed up today because our leader told us to." However, by the end of the session they allowed that since they knew more about drugs than anyone, being of course in the business, they would be delighted to instruct the staff of the Mass. Mental Health Center. (Get off it, man, you're freaking me out!)

Perhaps for a population of bikies, it is appropriate to think not so much of a school in the sense of teachers giving something to students but rather a school in which the students are the teachers and the teachers are the students. A mechanism may conceivably be set up in which there is an *exchange* of relevant information. If the subject is drugs, the relevant information is no doubt on the side of the bikies. But maybe there are subjects, important to bikies, in which the relevant information is on the side of the con- ventionally well-educated. Best of all there might be subjects which would induce each side to contribute something.

Bikies are very important to the youth of Jamaica Plain — at least in the poor white areas. They do indeed have a romantic aura. Many little kids want to grow up to be bikies. Bigger kids wish that they could join. Bikies can go anywhere. They are big shots in the drug rackets. They can have any woman they want. They fly across the countryside, out- running cops and straight people of all sorts. They are *brothers.* Cross one and the others may kill you. They are studiously wild, tough, and proudly dangerous. But at least one of the motorcycle clubs which I know, recognizing its charisma, is interested in the betterment of the youth of the community. The Red Emeralds. Some of the club members, with the active encouragement of their leader, have been helping Nick to run a better drop-in center. They wish to be mentors to the youth and, like Nick and Dick, to prevent kids, growing up on the streets, from going through what they did. On the other hand, some bikies scare the hell out of me. Although the rhetoric borders on standard New Left, the style is brutal, the romance is jackboot. Their appeal is that of the uniformed SS to the drifting youth of the Weimar Republic.

* * *

Martin Luther King's Birthday, January 15, 1970
I am old, and idealism and love and kids and freedom and learning to be Summerhill and Leicestershire are perpetrated on an innocent market. The young.
    Fraudulent.
               put them together and whathaveyougot?
               bippety boppety boo
               because they got no form
    Is it right to expect children to create the forms that have evolved for all these thousands and thousands and thousands of years? Choice is not what it's *all* about, although a component. The real problem is how in a crazily complicated scene to fit in, to make sense. Not to luxuriate in senselessness. It may be necessary to loosen a few screws, relax the moral code where it becomes absurd, but *without* one it is very lonely. Dangerous. Impossible for each of us to design separate new cultures. And hedonism deadens the taste buds.
    A school must be designed somehow to pass something useful on to the young that they in turn pass on embellished to their young. It must cumulate. And it must be valued for the sake of everyone. Certain things must be sacred and

carried in ritual even though manifestly senseless except that they allow us to verify ourselves as part of a larger entity. God is a metaphor for the society that must accept us or we go crazy. If the information, the skills, the rules, the rituals fail us, or if we can't comprehend them, or if we disvalue them or rationalize the myths, everybody dies. That is what is so frightening about a revolution which is not utopian; no context for thought. On the other hand, the romantic, the utopian revolution which adheres to an ideal is dangerous because whatever is in opposition is destroyed except for that little insecure inspirational asshole bureaucrat.

What is there left but cynicism?

And schools . . .

A school must first of all be a culture that is capable of defining who we are. It must allow children to grow by providing a rational milieu and an unambivalent voice which says "Yes" or "No."

If the larger culture for which the school is preparing the child is irrational, then of course there is no hope. To the extent that it is comprehensible, however, a school which is safe and predictable will prepare the child for chaos by providing small doses of chaos with intermittent success at cohering.

That is what is equally awful about both the crazy schools and the traditional urban public schools. Nothing can *happen* in either. Who is there to turn the kids on? Get them to want to reach out and grasp reality and learn to build with it as with clay?

It is not individual choice that is the measure. It is social value. Value to others. The group at first, then only as an instance of generalized others, meaning humanity as well as animals and plants — life. *Not* the life of a single individual. The life of *all* gives each immortality and permits us willingly to sacrifice for others because it is through them that we will continue.

("Says Joe I didn't die.")

You might even say that it is the duty of the school to teach children the value of sacrifice. It is necessary that the child learn that he cannot define himself except in social altruism. The school must teach that there is a reality outside of the single head which can be understood and controlled for the sake of us all.

Our uniqueness as individuals, deeply rooted, rather than superficial, depends paradoxically on how much a part of others we are at present and through history. The difference: between the American child who has never had a steady, loving, intact family and the old men of a traditional society where the family is the village and has been forever.

It may be argued that in preparing a child to live in a changing world we need a school based in change and infinite choice so that he can have plenty of practice in choosing. That makes choice a technical skill. "It will come with practice." The real problem is the *basis* on which to choose. Is it choice A that is consistent with what I believe or is it choice B? How do I know if I don't know what I believe?

A school must be able to make sense of the world, providing guidelines for the evolution of belief systems that are consistent with the basic principle of altruism and the culture of which the child is a part, however marginal at the moment. The particular variant of the generally accepted belief system that the child accepts is his own business. The major constraint is that it fit in somewhere.

Not so easy these days for a person of conscience. Solutions may need to be imaginative and may require considerable exploratory time before they are arrived at. But the process of exploration is okay as long as the goal is believed in. The process alone is nothing without a goal.

What I am saying is that schools need a theology. They must find a god. But you can't just do it like that. It has to be based in prior lives and in neighbors.

* * *

197

I read an article in *Atlas* about a Marxist priest in Brazil who is organizing revolutionary cadres among the peasants. Apparently there are a great many left-wing clerics in Latin America. Read about one Father Torres from Colombia who was killed in the struggle. Brave and fascinating men. They represent established, indeed exploitative, institutions and at the same time are leading the revolution.

I would like to do the same except that I have not put my life on the line; neither am I brave.

The focus of Latin American Revolutions is the United States, an external power, a foreign enemy. Everything is interconnected. But when *we* talk of "reforming" American education, we do not mean "exappropriating the exappropriators" or "throwing the foreign hordes into the sea." We mean instead that it is necessary to change the relationship between the school and the community it serves. Schools seem now designed to perpetuate an increasingly rigid class system by failing to educate the poor on the one hand, and on the other by training the rich to assume the reins of power. They do this in part by avoiding thought in favor of memory, ethics in favor of propaganda and God in favor of Santa Claus. Refusing to teach (or permit) underclass children to think can only serve to perpetuate the tenure of those presently in charge.

The Red priests achieve church reform by becoming martyred revolutionary leaders, emulating Christ. And they fight for those conditions necessary to the nurturance of social and individual morality — agrarian socialism and freedom from foreign domination. What is the larger context in which *we* operate or should operate? Who is *our* Christ? Dewey? Freud? Marx? Montessori? Lenin? Rousseau? Tolstoy?

Dissatisfied with American foreign policy, concerned with civil rights, power-wealth distribution, employment, housing, and schools, I consider myself an atheoretical, unprogrammatic good-guy. I do not think that an educator's thrust should be toward revolution, even though if he does his job well — that is, if he educates — the sum total of his efforts will be toward the furtherance of cataclysmic change.

One learns in order to gain control of the conditions and events that determine one's physical and spiritual existence. Even to know that my destiny is controlled externally, that I am at the mercy of a table of random numbers, a probability statistic, ultimately unmanageable, is precisely to achieve a kind of internal control — however perverse.

But where people have endlessly been exploited, where lives have not been permitted to flower, where arbitrary limits to self-realization have become traditional, to teach the possibility of knowing is precisely to foment revolt, to create violent dissent among the outcasts, the degraded . . . the exploited. When indignation is allowed, God help us all!

When indignation is forbidden, the devil take the government! The line between knowing and acting is not very firm.

* * *

I think that Jim Reed has been concerned about this knowing-acting dimension and has rightly perceived me as coming down too firmly on the side of the knower; not willing enough to take up the cudgels of battle — particularly on those fronts which count most to him — black leadership and male employment.

* * *

There is a real question in the purposive approach. When it comes to EDUCATION it simply may not be that proceeding in a straight line makes the most sense. One can, of course, say beforehand: "I will produce such and such a kind of child" and quite possibly through refined conditioning follow through precisely on target. But what if one cannot choose

199

between targets and selects them *all* instead? Suppose you say simplemindedly: "I want to produce a *full human being*"? Suppose you say that you want to produce people who, with dignity and grace, can be a part of the world and yet transcend it; can work and love and lead and follow and be alone and think as others do and yet can raise objections and can perform vitally? Well, it becomes too much! When the purpose is all purposes it gets crazy and maybe stupid. The structure of the program, the place, and the time make perhaps less difference than the attitude and the sense of transcendental, unspecific purpose. The goal of our program was grand, vague, and humanistic, and so our first task, ludicrously performed, was to demonstrate to ourselves, and secondarily to others, that we ourselves were human beings and should respect the humanity of the other guy.

* * *

March 15, 1970

Just read an article in the *Times* on Female Lib.

Intense, subtle, intricate feelings of oneness come about in the male-femaleness of each other. Take a family. How can someone external decide who is or isn't oppressed. It is only where there are no feelings of attachment, where people are glued together by an abstraction: habit, duty, tradition. ". . . to grind in the mill of an undelighted and servile copulation."

It is then that both are exploited, the weaker most visibly. Father, resting his ego on the fragile prop of occupation, is no less a victim than mother, roaring through the house on a vacuum cleaner in fierce control.

The master-slave allegory is amenable to radical words except when the system becomes only a blurred backdrop and the play is performed in intimacy. Character gets in the way. The house nigger is the master, etc.

200

Rhetoric doesn't ring true in the morning; the abstraction: unshaven, in pajamas.
Slogans contradict humanity.
Women should be treated as people. Of course.
Why not?
Everybody should be treated right.
Even me.
Revolutionaries are rigid.
They make *me* feel like an object. Not to be taken into account.
Robespierres and Stalins.
Shit on them.
Female lib is a cop-out on caring, protesting the untested constraint.

* * *

I just returned from Christmas in Ann Arbor with Mary's mother, sister, aunt, and a wide assortment of friends and relatives. Flew back home alone in order to get some writing done.

It's raining hard now and I can hear it on the roof and windows but it's dry and snug in my study and the radio is going. I am content. Ate at Moy Moy's alone with Melanie Klein barking and scratching at the door in the driving cold rain. She was left by herself for four days and is absolutely pathological about even a hint of continuing separation.

The house is quiet.

Grandma got a rugged bush for a tree but with the lights and decorations it looked nice. Michael and his cousins, Bobby and Jimmy, chased each other all over the house, laughing, screeching, and making pests of themselves. Alice, ladylike, appeared above that but the night before slept with her friend Jenny and squealed and giggled all night long. We had a marvelous turkey dinner at Aunt George's.

There were so many presents under the tree. Toys, sleds, clothes, gadgets. "Oh, thank you *so* much. Just *exactly* what I wanted. Oh, oh, oh, it's so *pretty!*" We couldn't open the presents until eight o'clock Christmas morning. Aunt Julie couldn't sleep for excitement. Uncle Ron, in his bathrobe, bleary-eyed, took pictures. Somebody asked Michael if he celebrated Chanukah. "I'm half Jewish and half Christian," he replied. "So I celebrate *all* the holidays!"

My wife believes in Santa Claus, I think. That is the essential religious difference between us. "Oh, open the damned presents anytime you feel like it," I tell the kids maliciously. She gets mad. The kids claim they wish I was right but they know their mother is. So they actually *don't* touch the presents until Christmas morning.

It's a nice custom in a way. Presents aren't the main thing. They are simply an occasion to bring the family together. And then they all go through their kindly ritual. Wrapping presents. Attaching notes about how they are from "Santa Claus" or "Daddy and Mom". And then at the appointed time, opening them with surprise and appreciation which is only partially manufactured.

I am a Jewish atheist but I wish that Christmas brought us close to God.

Any god.

And that the currency were something other than presents.

A certain amount of *things* are good. Kids should have toys and clothes — particularly toys. And people should have friends whose love is symbolized in a gift. But we have taken it to such excess that it loses pleasure, the delight of having just what you always wanted, the filling of a void.

We are gluttons. We gorge in banquet after banquet. No longer tasting with exquisite sensibility but stuffing our maws.

After the turkey at Aunt George's of which I had second helpings — white meat and dressing and potatoes, wine, apple

202

pie, and several cups of coffee — I was offered much the same on the plane. Landing in New York for a brief visit with my parents, a bowl of borscht was pushed at me — the cabbage soup kind — rich, pungent with black bread and some yogurt and a cup of coffee.

It loses all sense.

The poor. The limbless Vietnamese orphans. The ragged children of Jamaica Plain, huddled around a warm pusher or, better, around the gas stove in Nick's; the oven, stuffed with bricks, supplies the heat and the dryness. There is nothing but a few chairs and sofas taken from condemmed houses, found on the streets, too threadbare to have been stolen. My god, I thought, why does Michael need another sled? Another board game? Alice has so many dresses. And we couldn't think of anything for Grandpa Max because he has everything so we got him another burglar alarm. He has three. We are swimming in crap. Drowning. And it becomes us and we it.

The poor want to be like us in this respect. Fat. Give crap to the starving orphans. They already believe that they are unfavored because their homes are not floating in plastic. Help the unfortunate join the potlatch.

I suppose that's why we romanticize the poor. Because they have nothing. They can't be decadent in the same way that the rest of us are. Yet sadly, I suspect, that the poor wish they were. "Oh, to be fat, insensitive, gorged beyond health, reason, morality. To be bloated, to float above the rest, puking, shitting a few favors."

The dreams of the poor are not unlike ours, more so because they have less. Sex fantasies of a virgin. Excessive, maybe even a bit perverted, but not so unlike you and me for all that.

So why not simply *pray* at Christmas? For all of us. God damn.

* * *

203

Chapter Seven

VICTORY

A Little Entertainment: *John Henry*, **a Radio Play**

August 14, 1953; Camp Marcella (The New Jersey Camp for Blind Children)
When John Henry was a little baby
Sitting on his mammy's knee
He took a ten-pound hammer
And a little piece of steel
Said that hammer'll be the death of me, lord, lord
Said that hammer'll be the death of me . . .

This is the story of a man
A great big man
Who walked tall and straight
His granite head seemed to reach above the tree tops
His voice echoed across the valley when he talked
And made the whole earth tremble
But he was a man
Nothing but a man
His muscles were like steel bands
His black skin shone like velvet in the hot sun
While sweat rolled in rivers down his back
A working man
Who never stooped or scraped

As large as all the South
As tall as the Allegheny Mountains
But a man
Nothing but a man . . .
(I wondered about poor people when I was a child; about
blacks. I remember walking down the Bowery with my father.
"Why are these men sleeping in the street, in the hallways, in
the gutter? Are they dead?" My mother said, or was it someone else's mother, "Look at the colored man." I looked
expecting to see a rainbow man with green and harsh
orange and yellow and red — sort of like an awning and I was
disappointed to see an ordinary man, and sad because I didn't
get it. On the way to Miami the train stopped in a little town
and I went to the black toilet and everybody stared at me. . . .
Waterboy, gimmie a little drink, will ya, huh?
Man, I'm thirsty. That sun is hotter'n the devil's
own fire.

Here's your water, Jack

I'm so tired, so tired. I'd love to sit down for just
a minute. Just a minute.

Keep that hammer goin', boys

Take this hammer
Carry it to the captain
Take this hammer
Carry it to the captain
Take this hammer
Carry it to the captain
Tell him I'm goin'
Tell him I'm goin'

Some day I'm going to quit this job. Swinging this

twelve-pound hammer all day for fifteen years is
enough for any man. And what do I got to show
for it? Just up to the capt'n, that's what I'll do.
And you know what I'll tell him? I'll say,
"Capt'n, take my hammer 'cause I'm quittin'
this job. I don't want to see you, the hammer, nor
the whole C & O railroad no more."

You quit! That I gotta see! Who's goin' feed your
kids and shoe their pretty little feet? And how
about Annie? She comin' here to drive steel
while you sniff the flowers?

Boys, I just heard news that'll solve our problems.
Make things easier for all of us. Help do our work,
in fact.

What they got now, an automatic steel driving
machine?

Har har ha ha har har ha! An automatic steel
driving machine!

Don't laugh boys, don't laugh. Man from up North
come here yesterday. Saw the capt'n and he say:
"We got a drill here works by steam. It can drill
rock faster'n any man living. Just hitch it up,
light the fire under the boiler, get yourself a man
to run it and you're set. Easy and cheap."

Sounds good. Real easy. Nothing to do but push
buttons. No sweat. No aching muscles. Man, that's
for me.

Yeah, sounds great. Yeah. Yeah. Yeah.

206

Well, I don't know, fellows. It sounds good all right but I don't know. I don't rightly know. But it sure does sound good.

(May 2, 1962. I am beginning a diary. I intend simply to record the events and thoughts that may lead eventually to a better way of handling the job of school psychologist. It is a rat race of a job if there ever was one. We have impossibly large case loads and suffer from absurdly high expectations on the part of the school and the community. We are expected, for example, to diagnose and "cure" over two hundred children each year. In addition we are expected to advise teachers and principals and console parents and if necessary refer to other agencies, remaining, of course, in liaison with those agencies. It makes me sick to think of it. We don't think. We either rush around wildly or gripe in endless coffee breaks. We need to do research if for no other reason than that it may force us to look at what we're doing. I honestly don't think we know enough about psychotherapy yet to sell communities on our skill as agents of behavior change. However, I think that we know just about enough to become collaborators with the community in an effort to discover methods of predictably modifying human behavior and evaluating critically the direction of the change. More of this later. Right now I must get back to work.)

John! John! Get up, man! It's five-thirty already. You goin' to work or ain't you?

I'm comin' Polly. I'm comin'. Polly, you know what I told you the boys at the tunnel were saying yesterday?

You mean that steam drill?

Yes. Do you believe a machine can drive steel
faster'n a man?

Well. . . .

Polly, I'll tell you, I don't know about that
machine. It may make things easy and it may not.
But one thing is sure: If it can work faster'n a man,
steel driving won't be the same no more. Where'll
us hammer-whoppers be then? A few will push the
buttons on the machine and the rest will look for
work somewhere else or starve.

Don't worry, we'll always make out. Always have.
Coffee? Corn bread?

No . . . no. I ain't hungry.

Mornin', daddy. Mommy. Hey, daddy, is it true
what the kids tole us?

What's that?

Daddy says he can lick any steam drill and he says
he'll prove it too. Our daddy is the strongest man
in the whole world and there ain't no machine can
work better'n him.

What's that you been saying to folks, John?

I've been saying I'm mad and I ain't quitting my
hammer — never! Things is goin' to get bad if we
don't do something about them. I told the boys
yesterday that there ain't no machine nowhere
that's better'n a man. A man's a man. Made by
the good lord!

208

What do you aim to do then, John?

I'm going to beat that steam drill down. I'm going
to show the captain that no machine can outdrill
the best hammer man in the country. I'm going
to beat that steam drill or die trying.

* * *

(Memorandum to: Dean Sizer, et al. From Bob Belenky
and Jay Clark. October 11, 1965.

They will not be subjects in the traditional sense since
they will be told honestly of our purposes. Instead they
will be more like consultants and will afford us practice in
dealing on a colleague level with people ordinarily separated
from us by race, class, education, and age barriers.

In order to facilitate contact with the community, we
intend to hire Mr. James Reed, a bright, sensitive forty-five
year old Negro, who has many strengths which our program
needs. He is well respected within the Roxbury community
and has had previous successful work experiences with teen-
agers. As white university people, we felt that we would have
insurmountable difficulties being accepted by both the Negro
community and the white working class groups. This man
clearly can do what we can't. We would work with him, learn
from him, and in turn teach him what we know, seeking
thereby to develop a truly collaborative relationship. Maybe
some day we'll all write a book together.

It is to be expected that our program will grow in un-
foreseeable ways during the year.)

We're definitely going to put her on the job
Monday and boys, you never saw the likes of
this machine. It's as big as a house and it shines
so pretty — the brass pipes and all. And you should
hear her when she starts up — sounds like the

209

ground is like to open wide. She's a regular fire-
spitting, steam-sweating volcano, she is. She'll
make things real easy for you boys. And what's
more. . . .

Can she really drill faster than a man, Capt'n?

Faster than any man, living or dead.

Captain! *You are a liar!*

That's John Henry
Is he going to make his dare?
He's a fool if he tries
But look at them muscles on him. Man!
Capt'n, that ain't the truth you been telling us!

Your drill may be big
It may shine like a ball of fire
It may snort and roar like the Mississippi River
But it can't beat no man!
For twenty years I been swinging this ol' hammer
And my pappy done it before me.
What steam drill can tell you that?
Capt'n you get your steam drill.
Bring it 'round.
I'll work long side of it for as long as you say.
At the end of the time, you'll see
That old steam drill crying for its mammy.
John Henry is a steel-driving man!
There ain't none on this sweet earth can beat him
Be it made of flesh or iron!
And hear me boys! I swear
Before that steam drill beats me down
I'll die with a hammer in my hand!

Lord, lord!

Yes I'll *die* with a hammer in my hand!

There's lightning in John's eye when he talks.
I do believe his voice rocks them mountains.
There's a storm brewing for sure.
And it ain't going to lead to no good.

(September 22, 1968.
   Well, all the people at the party had been to Europe for the
summer and one guy spent a couple of weeks in Paris negotiating with the Viet Cong, for Christ sake! Another guy is an
architect and was holding forth about all the fucking schools,
prisons, and mental hospitals he's built which are so good that
recidivism rates have declined everywhere his magic wand was
wafted. Another guy is a couple of years younger than I
and already a major social scientist, gets invited to all sorts
of conferences, has tenure at a most elegant university,
spends ten weeks or more each summer at Martha's Vine-
yard, writes, publishes. I feel like a waste. Everyone comes
on so goddam jolly, friendly — indeed, flirtatious. I pull in.
I told Mary this morning that I want to start a great
residential program. Like a camp only much better. Year
around. And it could be a training, research, and service
place all rolled into one. In the country not too far from
Boston. Use orphans from all over the world as a residential
population. She felt that the family might not see me if I
got so involved.)

Stand back folks! Little boy, you're going to get
hurt if you stay there.

Aw, gee whiz!

211

Run along, I say. The contest of the century is
about to start. There on your left is the steam
drill — shiny and new-the greatest invention
since the cotton gin!

And on your right is your friend and mine, the
champion steel driver of the U.S. and A., husband
to Polly-Ann and father of four lovely children,
only man ever to swing two twenty-pound
hammers at one time. I give you — John Henry!!!

Hooray! Yay! Yay! You show 'em John! Atta go,
John! Yaaaay!!!

They say Capt'n bet a hundred dollars against him.
John ain't got a chance!
These mountains'll turn to gold afore he beats that
machine!
But he sure got guts to try!

When I fire this gun, the race will begin. Are you
ready up there in the steam drill?

Yes!

Are you ready, John?

Ready!

One . . .
Two . . .
Three . . .
(*Bang!*)

Oh, the Captain said to John Henry
"I believe this mountain's sinking in,"

212

John Henry said to the Captain, "Oh, my!
"Ain't nothing but my hammer sucking wind,
lord, lord
"Ain't nothing but my hammer sucking wind."

John Henry said to the people,
"Oh, friends, why don't you sing?
"I'm throwing twelve pounds from my hips on
down,
"Just listen to the cold steel ring, lord, lord
"Just listen to the cold steel ring."

John Henry told his captain
"Looka yonder what I see —
"Your drill's done broke and your hole's done
choke
"And you can't drive steel like me, lord, lord
"And you can't drive steel like me."

Hooray! Hooray! Yaaaaaaay!
The winner of the contest — JOHN HENRY!!!
Weeeee!! Yaaaaay! Hooraaaay!! Yipppeeee!!!

Polly, Polly come. I ain't going to last much
longer. Polly, I *beat* that steam drill. I beat her
down. Kids, come say so long to your pa. I'm
going now, but remember, your pa died with a
hammer like a man! I died a steel driving man . . .

Lord, lord . . .

He died a steel driving man . . .

John died on the mountains

And they prayed for his soul

213

And everyone who knew him cried
Everything was so quiet
Even the birds in the hills stopped singing
Because they missed the sound of John's hammer
When it made the cold steel ring. . . .
But this is not a sad story
Let's sing a song to John Henry
A happy song
To a man
Who showed us how big a man can be
Bigger than a steam drill of course
But taller than the sky
If he sets his mind to it. . . .
John Henry is dead
But somewhere deep inside
Of you
And me
He lives
And when we sing about him
We can hear his hammer in the wind
Even now
Listen. . . .

John Henry told his captain
"Well, a man ain't nothing but a man
"And before I let that steam drill beat me down
"I'll die with a hammer in my hand, lord, lord
"I'll die with a hammer like a man!"

(So what's the point already?)